JESUS ON DEATH ROW

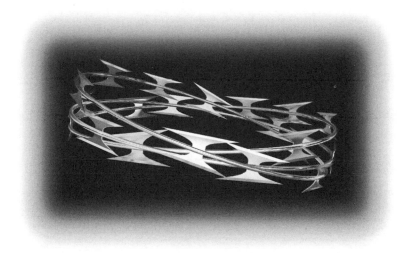

The Trial of Jesus
and
American Capital Punishment

MARK WILLIAM OSLER

Abingdon Press
Nashville

JESUS ON DEATH ROW
THE TRIAL OF JESUS AND AMERICAN CAPITAL PUNISHMENT

This book is printed on acid-free paper.

Library of Congress Cataloging-in-Publication Data

Osler, Mark William.
 Jesus on death row : the trial of Jesus and American capital punishment / Mark William Osler.
  p. cm.
 Includes bibliographical references and index.
 ISBN 978-0-687-64756-9 (hardback : alk. paper)
 1. Jesus Christ—Trial. 2. Jesus Christ—Crucifixion. 3. Capital punishment—United States I. Title.
 BT440.O85 2008
 232.96'2—dc22

                                                                    2008035294

09 10 11 12 13 14 15 16 17 18—10 9 8 7 6 5 4 3 2 1

MANUFACTURED IN THE UNITED STATES OF AMERICA

To my family, and in particular to my mother,

PHYLLIS OSLER,

who taught me to love books, and to my father,

JOHN OSLER,

who taught me to see beauty and meaning everywhere

CONTENTS

ACKNOWLEDGMENTS

This book would not have been possible without the additional support of Baylor Law School and its dean, Brad Toben. Throughout, the book reflects the advice of the members of Seventh and James Baptist Church, particularly the members of the Roundtable Sunday School class, which included my primary writing mentors, Bob and Mary Darden. Those who inspired or assisted me in other ways include Susan Artinian, Dr. Raymond Bailey, Larry Bates, Ed Bray, Tom Brooke, Nancy Bryan, Steven Chanenson, Robert Cochran, Adina Coman, Matthew Cordon, Ashley Cruseturner, Hon. Jan E. Dubois, Melissa Essary, Tom Featherston, Hope Friewald, David Garland, Amy Garrou, Terry Ging, Hulitt Gloer, Linda Gradel, Mark Hauck, Lane Haygood, Kris Helge, Misty Keene, Linda Lampert, Anne Lewis, Michelle Lowery, Hon. Jeffrey Manske, Barbara and Hugh Marlow, Blaine McCormick, David Meadors, Jonathon Nuechterlein, Randall O'Brien, Craig Pankratz, Florencia Rueda, Rory Ryan, Ann Scarff, Michael Schwartz, Jami Symank, Nicole Tingelstad, Katherine White, and Pat Wilson.

Portions of the book were written at Middlebury College and the Yale Club of New York, and I thank the library staffs of those institutions for their hospitality and assistance. Finally, I must thank Robert Ratcliff and the other editors at Abingdon Press, who not only gave this book a chance but also made it much better than it would have been without their help.

INTRODUCTION

In 2001, I was a new professor at a conservative Christian law school in Texas, having left a career as a federal prosecutor in Detroit. I loved teaching and the eagerness of my students to learn and become lawyers. My colleagues supported my varied interests, and I was thrilled to find myself in the midst of a community of scholars, giving me lunchtime access to experts in theology, sociology, philosophy, business, and the sciences. It was as if my mind had been freed and I had been placed in a garden of intellectual delight.

Flush with the excitement of these heady times, I set after an ambitious goal: to juxtapose the story of Christ with the reality of capital punishment in the state of Texas. Specifically, I wanted to conduct the capital trial of Christ, under Texas rules, in a Baptist church in Waco, Texas. I was to be the prosecutor, my colleague Bill Underwood agreed to be the defense attorney, and the congregation would be the jury over the course of four Sundays.

In retrospect, perhaps it wasn't such a great idea for an untenured professor at a Baptist school to prosecute Christ. In a Baptist church. On Sunday. I suppose it might have been a mistake to have railed against the dangers of Christ in my closing argument or to urge a verdict for the ultimate punishment before a jury containing many of those who would later judge my application for tenure.

It was no mistake. The experience was riveting as it exposed the sharp contrast between the central narrative of Christianity and the affection of most Texans for the death penalty. The jury selection was intense and troubling as we weeded out those strongly opposed to the death penalty from the potential jury (as required by Texas law). Two of those who remained on the jury, it turned out, had previously served on juries that had actually condemned men to die. One might have expected it to be difficult to fit the ancient story into the modern rules, but it wasn't; in fact, the present Texas procedures proved to be remarkably similar to the process that Christ encountered. In the end, after a lengthy and combative debate among the jurors, the jury was hung.

That experience, while perhaps a poor career choice, spurred a thought that has since driven me in my analysis of law—the legal issues raised by the story of Jesus Christ, defendant, are many of the same issues we face today. The death penalty, certainly, but also habeas procedures; forfeiture of a criminal's assets to the state; the role of humiliation in punishment; the use of paid informants; the prevalence of interagency task forces; the role of emotional appeals—each of these not only is part of the contemporary debate over criminal law, but was raised in the biblical accounts of the trial of Jesus.

Principal among these legal issues is capital punishment. The death penalty has been a controversial topic for generations and seems to be almost immune from consensus. Fewer states are actually executing prisoners, and within the United States the majority of executions are in my home of Texas. My friend Doug Berman, who teaches sentencing law at Ohio State, often and correctly points out that the debate over capital punishment too often obscures other issues within sentencing that affect far more people. Nonetheless, it is an important national discussion in that our use of the death penalty, and the debate around it, raises issues at the heart of American principles and self-definition. In a way that is increasingly rare when we talk about political issues, both sides in the discussion of capital punishment articulate principles rather than positions or insults.

Not that this makes it easy; the contradictions and confusion of principles run deep. On the one hand, we justify capital punishment as deterring crime, but on the other, we hold executions in secret chambers hidden from public view. It has been some fifty years since Albert Camus commented that if our society really meant for the death penalty to deter crime, "it would exhibit the heads. Society would give executions the benefit of the publicity it

2

generally uses for national bond issues or new brands of drinks."[1] Still, the machinery proceeds in secret, not on pay-per-view. At every turn, it seems, similar conflicts arise over our sense of what is right.

My purpose in writing this book is not to rehash policy arguments that have already been made, however. Instead, I start from the simple observation that many of those involved in the debate over the death penalty are professing Christians, a faith that has at its very core a capital sentence—that of Jesus Christ. Perhaps most prominently, Presidents Bill Clinton and George W. Bush strongly supported and expanded the use of the death penalty while both proclaimed a faith whose primary public symbol, the cross, is itself the representation of an instrument of execution.

Like nearly all of those who discuss the death penalty, Bush and Clinton do not refer and have not referred to the experience of Jesus Christ. In a nation where 85 percent of the population identifies itself as Christian, the debate over capital punishment and other criminal issues is necessarily going to be largely among Christians. For Christian participants in the debate, the troubling account of Jesus Christ as a criminal defendant should be a part of the discussion.

It is odd that the experience of Christ is not *already* a part of that discussion. After all, when Christians around the world gather to celebrate the Eucharist, consider what the communion table represents: the Last Supper, which was the last meal of a man who knew he would be executed. Much has been written about the last meals of modern capital defendants; what a convict chose for that last meal is often described in newspaper accounts of an execution. But how often do we make any connection between the two?

In the following pages I will sort out what happened to Jesus and hold it up to the experiences of criminal defendants in the United States today. At several levels, there is a significant match. At the surface, there is a simple correspondence between some of the criminal procedures used then and now, such as arraignment, the use of confidential informants, jury trials with a jury that does not represent the population, and posttrial procedures. At a deeper level, too, we see a consistent desire to humiliate the defendant, some-thing a convict in America would easily recognize. At the level of motivation as well, those seeking the execution of Christ seem to have been driven by something very close to our ascendant national goals of retribution and incapacitation as methods of social control.

Researching and writing this book caused me to challenge America's use of the death penalty based on the lessons to be drawn from the experiences of Christ as a defendant. This rethinking was as much emotional, in empathizing with Christ, as it was intellec-tual. One thing that makes the Gospels so relevant and meaningful to the modern world is that they are an emotional narrative, and we live in a world where we are surrounded by such narratives—we watch them on television, pay ten dollars to see storytelling movies, and snap up novels. Well-written stories bring fascinating charac-ters into our lives and lead us to care about them. The skillful writer crafts these characters carefully so that they will be appealing and likable, even heroic. Most Christians believe that God wrote the story of Christ on earth, the story that not just defines but created the Christian faith. Shouldn't it matter that God, then, created his hero as a criminal defendant. The fact that God's son came to Earth as a man subjected to capital punishment seems to reveal God's intent that we care about not only that man but also that process. The more we focus on that story of Jesus, the more the idea of cap-ital punishment becomes troubling. We care that Jesus was sub-jected to unfairness, cruelty, and hate, and as I examine in the following chapters, the process to which Jesus was subjected is not so different from our modern criminal justice routines.

For me, this example of Christ is but one of a number of reasons that the death penalty is not compatible with the Christian faith. Although this book primarily relates the experiences of Christ rather than his teachings, those teachings were remarkably straight-forward in condemning the death penalty. In John 8, Jesus was asked to opine on a lawful execution that was about to occur. There was no suggestion that the defendant was innocent, or that the crime was minor by the standards of the day. Jesus did not shrug his

4

shoulders, summarily conclude that the death penalty was necessary or approved in the Old Testament, and walk away.

Rather, he challenged the gathered crowd: a person without sin should cast the first stone of the stoning. Famously, no one did. They did not have the moral authority to execute another person, even when human law called for it. Could his teaching be any clearer? Jesus came upon the death penalty, about to be conducted, and stopped it. Imagine if he had come upon an abortion about to be committed and condemned it—I don't doubt that many would take that as an unambiguous moral statement.

I am not qualified to interpret the story further, though I find it quite powerful. Rather, my task is to look at the Jesus who was investigated, charged, tried for a crime, and sought posttrial relief. I am not a theologian, and in these pages I don't pretend to be one. I am a former prosecutor and a law professor who is intimately familiar with the process of modern criminal law and the issues within that law. I read the Bible as a layperson, not as an expert in Greek or Hebrew or the history of the Bible's interpretation. This viewpoint has a significant effect on my reading of the Gospel, and on the differences between this book and analyses of the trial of Christ by theologians. One significant difference is that I do not, in these pages, seek to analyze the authenticity of various passages within the Bible. Yes, I am aware that the Gospels were written after the time of Jesus, that Mark came first and John was written last; I know that some theologians question the authenticity of John 8, which I just quoted. Were I to address each of these debates instead of simply looking to the story told in the gospel, I would become nothing more than a third-rate, unqualified theologian.

Instead, I have chosen to work with the Gospel accounts of Jesus' death as a single narrative. For example, I have drawn from various Gospels where a story appears in one and not the others, where they are not in direct conflict. Many biblical scholars, including perhaps the late Raymond Brown (on whom I have relied greatly in writing this book), would accuse me of harmonizing the Gospels— that is, reading them as fitting together rather than focusing on the distinctive voice of each Gospel writer. I accept this criticism, but do not apologize for this approach. The church reads the Gospels as a diverse, yet unified, telling of the story of Jesus and its meaning for us. In these pages I have sought to do the same.

Also, I am not concerned here with whether the trial of Christ was consistent with Roman law or Jewish law of that time. Others have dealt with those topics better than I could. Instead, I want to look at Christ's experience, singular though it may have been, as a way to examine our modern processes in a new light.

Finally, I realize that it may seem odd or even offensive to some readers to use the life of Christ to analyze a process that today is almost always used in cases involving murder. Yet Christ himself invited us to do exactly that. In Matthew 25, Jesus talked of those who fail to help those who are naked or sick or in prison. In talking about those in prison, he said to his followers, "Truly I tell you, just as you did not do it to one of the least of these, you did not do it to me" (Matt 25:45). To some, the "least of these" means poor people, and I would agree. It also means the convicted criminal in prison, to whom Christ specifically referred. Like many of Christ's teachings, this one is hard to accept. Because of the role that Christ plays in the faith as a singular Messiah, he is at the opposite end of the spectrum of morality from the killer. But if we ignore the lessons to be drawn from Jesus' life because of his singular role in history, we lose the power and humanity of those stories that have animated the faith for centuries and informed the poetry of our heroes.

Thus, I have no problem with equating the hated, the guilty, even the imprisoned and reviled killer with Christ, for it is at Christ's invitation that I compare my society's treatment of the "least of these" with that of Christ himself.

CHAPTER ONE

THE STORY OF JESUS CHRIST, DEFENDANT

We live in a culture obsessed with criminal law. Television programs every night of the week show lawyers and investigators at work, trying cases and unraveling the complexities of a wide variety of crimes. Scores of movies also focus on criminal law, even creating entire realms of crime-solving in an alternative reality that includes superheroes.

Beyond fictionalized entertainment, there are few news stories with the long-term staying power of the prosecution life cycle: a juicy crime, arrest, trial, and sentence. Only a handful of stories have captured the public imagination in the past generation in the way that the arrest and trial of O. J. Simpson did, and it is hard to find a national news outlet that doesn't rely heavily on high-profile criminal cases as a mainstay for programming. From the trial of Martha Stewart through round-the-clock coverage of horrific terrorist acts, the news channels echo the fictional television dramas in their obsession with criminal law, creating news based on "celebrity justice" when no truly significant case is available to talk about. The saturation of our culture with true and untrue stories from the field of criminal law is nearly complete.

But why? Criminal law is but a small part of the field of law. On my faculty of twenty-four professors, just two of us teach criminal law courses. How, then, is criminal law able to so completely capture the imagination of our culture? The reason is simple—

compelling stories. We love to hear about the multiple, intertwined stories of the criminal defendant, the prosecutor, the police, and the jury. The criminal case has all of the requisites of an epic tale built right in, starting with the accusation of a gross moral failure. Throw in the presence of sex and violence, the search for truth, and multiple versions of events to create uncertainty, and a compelling tale is guaranteed.

These stories drew me into the practice of law and into criminal prosecution. To those of us who turn by hand the gears of criminal justice, it is these stories, the unremitting flood of tragedy, that enliven us, that make us wake up before dawn the day of trial, that wear us down emotionally, and that eventually erode the senses like drops of water over rock.

Perhaps it should come as no surprise, then, that the story at the center of the faith affirmed by 85 percent of Americans is set in the realm of criminal law, replete with the cycle of investigation, arrest, trial, and appeal familiar to even the most casual television viewer. Somehow, though, we don't make the connection. I was a prosecutor for five years, attending church the entire time, and I never contemplated that my vocation and faith had a strange and strong narrative link. While Christians focus on Jesus Christ, Savior and Jesus Christ, Teacher, and some now urge us to consider the possibility of Jesus Christ, Father and Jesus Christ, Husband, we have largely ignored what is so thoroughly described in the Bible: Jesus Christ, Defendant.

The truth is that, to a remarkable degree, the story of Christ replicates the very structures that shape criminal law today. Even more compellingly, the same troubling issues raised by Jesus' case are still with us and are at the center of some of our most vigorous moral debates. For example, academics and others have focused recently on the problems associated with a system of investigation that relies heavily on confidential informants who provide information to the police for money. A new debate? Hardly. Judas's thirty pieces of silver, given for snitching on Jesus, are one of the most compelling images of the Bible.

One significant difference between Christ's trial and modern criminal practice is that Jesus was prosecuted by religious leaders, while our legal system is often described as secular. However, we must remember that the religious leaders who prosecuted Jesus had an important political role, as was exemplified in the trial of Christ. In that place and time the line between religion and government was sometimes hard to discern, and those who placed themselves in positions of religious authority often sought to exert political authority as well.

The modern criminal case has several stages, each of which presents a different challenge and cast of characters. The same can be said of the experience of Christ as a criminal target and defendant. I will start by briefly describing those stages as an overview. Then I will fully develop each stage, the structure of the modern case and the process faced by Christ, in the following chapters.

The Investigation

As a prosecutor, I loved putting together cases, loved the challenge of leading a team of investigators in getting to the truth and bringing wrongdoers to justice. It was intensely satisfying to work out the puzzle of a conspiracy or to identify the man or woman who was truly receiving the benefits of a crime.

I worked with investigators from more agencies than I can remember, an amalgam of initials and names already well known in the popular imagination—the IRS, the FBI, the Secret Service, the ATF, the DEA, the Detroit police, the state police, and the INS. In starting off a case or in locating defendants, these investigators interacted with the defendants themselves. They bought drugs from the defendants, had conversations on the street, followed them home, and made a point of knowing the lives of those they would arrest. Part of that interaction, especially undercover work, is often an attempt to get the target of the investigation to do something, such as sell drugs, while the officers are watching and evidence can be gathered.

Similarly, the Bible tells the story of Christ as the target of investigation, who had frequent contact with his accusers prior to his arrest. They encountered him, challenged him, and monitored his actions. In the last weeks of his life, it seems, he was almost constantly under surveillance by the authorities who would eventually charge him. Time and again, the Pharisees and scribes tried to get Jesus to say or do something that they could take to the Roman authorities as proof of criminal activity. Like narcotics officers with a wad of money to buy marijuana, they were gathering evidence they could use against one they already suspected.

The Confidential Informant

In my cases, the target of an investigation frequently was hard to find. Not surprisingly, people who do illegal things often keep it quiet and stay out of the public view. Generally, the more significant the crime, the more likely this is to be true. As some criminals describe it, they want to keep things "inside the box," or within the circle of people who are involved. The criminal's desire for secrecy and wariness of outsiders are part of what make confidential informants and cooperating defendants so valuable to investigators. Confidential informants and cooperating defendants are enticed by the government to provide information about crimes they know are occurring. Confidential informants are paid, some quite handsomely, while cooperating defendants hope to receive a break in their own cases.

Informers of either type are usually involved in illegal activity, as would be expected, since that is how they get information from "within the box." Sometimes prosecutors tell juries, "You don't find swans swimming in the sewage," to explain the use of informants. To know what is going on in the muck, you need someone who is already there.

For example, one of my cases was made possible only by the cooperation of such a person inside the ring. Our informant, who had a history of low-level criminal activity, was working with a student at the University of Michigan who was preparing to print large amounts of counterfeit money using a computer. The student was very, very good at his task, and he was so careful that he started by counterfeiting one-dollar bills, which he used to test their ability to fool change machines. The student had assembled an unusual group of conspirators to further his plot, including a fellow student to help with the production, a real estate agent to aid in the distribution of the counterfeit bills into the community, and a cab driver, our informant, to help with minor tasks and transportation. The cab driver contacted the Secret Service about the plot before it reached fruition, hoping to get a break in another case and cash for his efforts. This informant aided us in many ways, including the tip about when and where all of the conspirators would be assembled so that we could conduct an efficient search and arrest.

The circle of Jesus' trust, of course, was not a ragtag band of college students, but the twelve apostles who surrounded and aided him. Much of what they did remained secret because Jesus was well aware that the authorities were monitoring him. And, like the cab driver, one of those from within the circle went to the authorities to provide information leading to Jesus' arrest. Intriguingly and typically, it was not the authorities who sought out Judas, but Judas who sought out the authorities. Like the cab driver, Judas tipped off the authorities about when and where all of the conspirators would be assembled for search and arrest. For that, he was paid thirty silver coins, and he has remained a despised figure in the public imagination for nearly two thousand years.

Strategic Arrest

Information provided by informants often leads to the stage after investigation, the arrest. Once investigators are ready to make an arrest in a case, they generally won't just send an agent over to the defendant's house to pick up him or her. Arrests are necessarily strategic, to serve several goals. Primary among these goals are gathering additional evidence and reducing the chance of violence or escape at the time of arrest.

In furtherance of this second goal, the arrests in my investigations were often made at six in the morning when the defendant was usually asleep and alone. That better enabled the agents to surprise the target and minimized the chance of being shot or hurt. The power of darkness gave the agents a great advantage.

Those arresting Jesus were certainly strategic in their actions, for the same reasons the police I worked with planned ahead. The authorities considered, for example, arresting Jesus during the Passover festival, but chose not to out of fear that the followers of Jesus might riot (Mark 14:2). Instead, the authorities elected to come at night in order to minimize the role of the apostles and Jesus' other followers. Intriguingly, Jesus seemed to have known their plan, and Matthew 26 describes his efforts to keep his followers awake through the night.

Jesus also knew exactly what a strategic arrest was. He confronted the officers with their contrivance, noting that "when I was with you day after day in the temple, you did not lay hands on me. But this is your hour, and the power of darkness!" (Luke 22:53).

Violence at the Arrest

If one chooses to work in the field of criminal law, one assumes a heightened risk of suffering violence. While that broadly is true, the risk is not the same for all players on the side of the prosecution. There is a significant risk for those at the bottom of the investigative organizations—patrol officers, new agents, and those from low-status agencies. Overwhelmingly, they are the ones who get shot. As with the military, those who make the strategic choices are not usually the ones who take the greatest risks of physical harm. Rather, it tends to be poor and working-class persons on both ends of the guns when law enforcement comes into contact with criminals.

Though many people appear to have been involved in the arrest of Jesus, the interloper with the lowest status, a slave named Malchus, had his ear lopped off by Simon Peter. As always, Jesus showed mercy to poor people, even when they were present only to arrest him. Before leaving with his captors, he touched Malchus and healed him of the wound inflicted by his apostle (Luke 22:51).

The Initial Appearance

A criminal's initial appearance or arraignment is one of the simplest proceedings in the criminal case. The process of bringing the defendant before a magistrate judge to be informed of the charges is called an initial appearance if the arrest is on a complaint, and an arraignment if it follows an indictment by the grand jury. Once the charge is read at this kind of proceeding, the defendant is allowed to enter a plea on the charge. One might think there are two possible answers to this question of whether the defendant is guilty or not: yes or no. In contemporary practice, however, the most common outcome is for the defendant to stand mute and say nothing. In these instances, the judge typically enters a plea of not guilty on behalf of the defendant based on his or her silence, and the defendant proceeds to trial.

This bit of Kabuki theater seems to have been followed almost precisely in the case of Christ. Before going to trial, according to John 18, Jesus was sent to Annas, a high priest. He questioned Jesus about the charge of blasphemy, and Jesus responded essentially by standing mute, saying, "Why do you ask me? Ask those who heard what I said to them; they know what I said" (John 18:21). Like the defendant arraigned in an American court, Jesus declined to claim guilt or innocence, and left the prosecution to its proofs.

The Last Meal of the Condemned

It is almost a set piece. In press accounts of executions, there is a near ritualistic description of what the condemned person chose for the last meal, usually some simple plate: steak, potatoes, a chocolate brownie. Perhaps we find this detail so compelling because it is a part of the process that is familiar to us, choosing our favorite foods. Or perhaps we focus upon it because its very simplicity makes the condemned person seem more real.

At the time of the Last Supper, Christ knew that he was to die before he ate again. In arranging the meal, Jesus sent out his disciples to find a specific man, and they were to say that Christ's "time is near" (Matt 26:18). At that meal, the Last Supper, he told them, "I will never again drink of the fruit of the vine until that day when I drink it new in the kingdom of God" (Mark 14:25). As with condemned persons in modern-day American prisons, that last meal is made real and human, even amidst the mists of transubstantiation, by the bare simplicity of bread and wine. In both our prisons and the upper room where the Last Supper was held, the meal is a feast not because of what is served, but because of the facts surrounding that food.

The Provision of a Trial

The proceeding before the council at which Caiaphas prosecuted Jesus had all the trappings of a trial. The fact that there was a trial at all is an important marker because it invites the consideration of the process as a criminal case. To a trial lawyer, the dynamics of the event were those of a trial—the uncertainty of it, the impact of emotion, and the troubling credibility judgments that the jury was forced to make.

The Gospels thoroughly and compellingly described the problems with the witnesses, most of whom lacked credibility in their eagerness to testify at Christ's trial. When I was a prosecutor, there was perhaps one element in my arsenal of evidence more troubling than a reluctant witness—an overeager witness. People are motivated to testify for the government by a variety of factors, ranging from simple vindictiveness toward the defendant to the desire of cooperating defendants to please the prosecutor in order to get a better deal for themselves. The very real danger with such motivated witnesses is that they tend to say things that they believe will most likely result in a conviction rather than tell the simple truth.

As a result, such witnesses can present testimony that then conflicts with that of other witnesses, or even the chronology of events presented in the government's opening statement.

Jesus' prosecutor, Caiaphas, faced the dilemma of the overmotivated witness. When asked individually what Jesus' blasphemy was, they made different claims about what it was, exactly, that Jesus had said (Mark 14:59). The Gospels made a point to describe both the problem (their eagerness) and the result (conflicting testimony), the same danger and reality we sometimes see manifested in trials today.

A myth propagated by television accounts of criminal law is that defendants almost always take the stand on their own behalf and try to explain away the charges. In fact, in many, if not most, cases that go to trial the defendant does not testify on his or her own behalf, on the advice of the defense attorney. The defense attorney might have made that recommendation because letting an untrained speaker allocute is risky, or because keeping the defendant off the stand will prevent the admission of prior crimes into evidence. In other cases, it may simply be that the best defense is to leave the government to its proofs.

The Gospels told somewhat different stories about what Jesus said in the course of his trial. In the Gospel of Luke, Jesus was asked, "Are you, then, the Son of God?" His simple response was nothing more than a requirement that the authorities provide proof: "You say that I am" (Luke 22:70). That, essentially, is the statement made by each defendant who does not take the stand, but leaves the government to its proofs.

An Emotional Closing Argument for the Prosecution

By the end of a trial, the prosecutor has a good idea of the strength of his or her case. If the witnesses have been clear, honest, and consistent, and each element has been proved beyond a reasonable doubt on the face of the evidence, the government's closing argument will be a logical statement describing that evidence and asking for a guilty verdict. Sometimes, though, things go wrong. Witnesses fail to say the right thing or mumble; evidence goes awry; the defendant does not testify as the prosecutor expected. In that situation, closing argument is likely to be somewhat more fiery. To engage the members of the jury with the facts going to guilt, the prosecutor will urge them to bring their passions, as well as their logic, to bear.

It seems that Caiaphas found himself in such a spot by the end of the trial of Christ. His witnesses failed him, the defendant left him to his proofs, and the nature of the blasphemy remained somewhat unclear. Like prosecutors everywhere, Caiaphas did his best to save the case and pulled out the fireworks, working himself into such a frenzy that he tore his clothes as he urged the jury to execute the defendant for his crimes. And as has often been the case in Texas, engaging the fears of the jury was good enough for a conviction.

Appeal

For the trial attorney, appeal is anticlimax. For the appellate attorney, it is the whole world. On appeal, the judge's actions are reviewed for consistency with the requirements of the law. The defendant can seek to have his or her case retried or to be released. The great majority of appeals in the United States are unsuccessful; in my home state of Texas the reversal of a conviction is so rare that when one occurs, it often becomes front-page news. In part, the reason is that the appellate judges, like the trial court judges, are elected, and in Texas the way to be elected is to be tough on crime.

What happened to Jesus after his trial tracks what today we would call an appeal. He was taken in chains to Pilate, who was the Roman prefect for the area. Pilate reviewed the evidence in the case, and apparently, he did not see much justification for the conviction. Luke 23:4 reports that Pilate was not inclined to favor the authorities, saying, "I find no basis for an accusation against this man." Even then, perhaps with one eye on the politics of the moment much in the manner of elected appellate judges, Pilate declined to reverse the conviction and free the prisoner.

The Habeas Petition

The writ of habeas corpus has been carried into American law from its British predecessor. The writ came from a time in which the king, the lords, and the church maintained their own justice systems and jails. Often, the imprisonment of a citizen by the king, by a lord, or by the church was challenged by the court of another of the three. In that instance, the prisoner sought a writ of habeas corpus, which was issued by the court and ordered that the jailer "show the body" and free him. If the court he petitioned had enough political power and issued this writ, he was freed.

In our modern system, the writ of habeas corpus similarly operates very often (but not exclusively) as a creature of our system of separate sovereigns, the federal government and the states. Once they have exhausted a state's process, state prisoners petition for writs of habeas corpus in the federal courts, asking that they be freed because of mistakes made by the state court at trial or sentencing. These petitions usually must be made after appeal is completed. In capital cases, habeas petitions are almost always pursued through the entire system of federal courts by those condemned to die by the courts of their home state.

Jesus, too, was given a hearing by a separate sovereign, according to the Gospel of Luke. In an account found only in that Gospel, Pilate sent Jesus to Herod for further consideration. Though the relative responsibilities of Herod and Pilate are a matter of controversy in some circles, it can safely be said that they represented separate sovereigns, with Pilate a direct representative of Rome, and Herod a local ethnic leader of Judea. Like state and federal officials, Pilate and Herod had overlapping responsibilities, and certain issues (such as what to do with Jesus) would sequentially come before both of them. Thus, it is fair to consider Jesus' appearance before Herod as the rough equivalent of a habeas petition passing first through the state and then the federal system. Jesus' habeas petition was unsuccessful, like those of most American prisoners. Herod simply sent Jesus back to Pilate (Luke 23:11).

Then, as now, civil authorities were reluctant to reverse even the most extreme and important failures of process. Though both Pilate and Herod might have suspected Jesus was innocent, he was not freed. Convicts in the United States, too, have often found that the standards they must meet in seeking a new hearing have little to do with actual innocence once an initial conviction has been obtained by the government. Instead, they must deal with judges who are inclined, like Herod, to let an execution proceed.

Clemency Refused

In the American capital punishment drama, one of the more compelling bits of theater is the request for clemency, pardon, commutation, or a stay of execution submitted to the governor, often at the last minute. We are familiar with the press accounts of these requests, which often describe the amount of time that the governor spent pondering the decision.

Jesus' last-minute clemency hearing was particularly poignant and dramatic. There was a tradition that at the Passover festival: the Roman authorities would release a local prisoner condemned to die—a pardon. The decision was in the hands of the Roman representative, Pilate, and he appeared to have still been inclined to find Jesus innocent. Pilate called together the leaders and the people, and he offered to release Jesus as part of this tradition, but the crowd urged him instead to release a murderer and insurrectionist named Barabbas. Pilate did so, and Jesus' last hope slipped away (Mark 15:6-15).

Humiliation of the Defendant

Visitors to an American court who happen to see a nontrial appearance by a defendant (that is, an initial appearance, an arraignment, a motion or plea hearing, or a sentencing) are often surprised by the dress of the defendant. No longer do defendants wear the stereotypical prison stripes or street clothes. Rather, those who are in custody, men and women, usually appear in court wearing ill-fitting orange or pink jumpsuits or scrubs. On their feet are the most primitive flip-flops, regardless of the weather. This manner of dress is accepted because it is inexpensive, and because the certain side effect of dressing a man in a pink jumpsuit, his humiliation, is seen as a necessary and good part of the process.

Such humiliation was a part of the story as well, including the manner of dress allowed Christ once he became a defendant. Part of the story of Christ's encounter with Herod was Herod's response to Jesus, who refused to answer the leader's questions. Luke 23:11 reported, "Even Herod with his soldiers treated him with contempt and mocked him; then he put an elegant robe on him, and sent him back to Pilate." Clearly, the elegant robe was a part of the mockery heaped on a man accused of falsely claiming to be a king, as noticeable and wrong as the pink jumpsuit of today.

The Method of Execution

Jesus was executed with the use of a horrible process that few would advocate today. He was hung on a cross and left to die as gravity did the work of the executioner, until the very weight of his body caused him to perish. To the credit of our society, we have sought increasingly humane forms of execution, leaving behind beheading, hanging, and electrocution in most jurisdictions.

However, the newer methods, including the dominant modern technique of lethal injection, are not without their problems. The method makes it impossible to know what the process is like for the executed person, and so any assumption that this is a more humane method is simply that—an assumption. Sometimes, too, it seems to cause real agony.

Intriguingly, this modern method of lethal injection has three separate components. First, an anesthetic is injected. Once that has taken effect, a second injection is made, designed to disable and paralyze the body. Only after this has taken effect is the third drug administered; it is the killing dose. These steps mirror the steps in Christ's execution: he was first offered wine and myrrh to dull his senses; then disabled as he was bound to the cross; and finally killed as the support for his feet was removed (or never provided at all). He died as the modern prisoner does—sedated, unable to struggle, and helpless.

Forfeiture

A secret revolution has gone on beneath the surface of U.S. criminal law. Over the past twenty years, many criminal justice organizations have found that they can finance themselves largely from the assets of the criminals they arrest. The process of seizing the possessions belonging to defendants can be relatively simple and very lucrative. There are three types of forfeitures—administrative, civil, and criminal—and all three can be used in conjunction with the criminal case. Administrative forfeiture, where a defendant fails to lay a proper claim to his property, is the easiest. Civil forfeiture, in which a civil lawsuit is filed against the property itself, is more complex. Most difficult of all for the state is criminal forfeiture, in which the forfeiture action is made a part of the criminal trial. Not surprisingly, most forfeitures are civil or administrative.

And what happens to the money received from the defendants? It is divided among the agencies involved in the case as they agree. As one might expect, this process creates unusual and sometimes improper incentives in the exercise of discretion; those making arrest and charging decisions certainly know that by prosecuting defendants with available assets, there will be a financial benefit to the investigating agencies, regardless of the relative culpability of those defendants.

By all accounts, Jesus was a man of few possessions. But those few possessions were not given to his family or to his followers. Rather, they were divided among the soldiers who crucified him. They could not divide his tunic, so for that part of the forfeiture, they drew lots (John 19:23-25).

Jesus did not kill a police officer or murder a child, as many of those on death row have done. To a Christian such as myself, his life was faultless. Nonetheless, my point here and in the rest of this book in drawing out the similarities between the procedure that Christ faced and our criminal procedure today is not to compare Christ with the murderer, but to compare the society that executed him with our own.

If God is the author of the story of Jesus on earth, and that story contains lessons for contemporary men and women, then it must mean something that so much of the heart of that story is about criminal law. If we treat our prisoners in the same way that Jesus was treated, then the Christians among us must ask if that comports with our faith, and struggle with the answer. The fact that this struggle may be difficult, contrary to our easiest instincts, and unpopular hardly distinguishes it from the other harsh challenges presented by a true faith. A God, after all, who demands sexual fidelity, who decries wealth, and who requires humility even in the mighty, seems like the kind of God who would also trouble our hearts as we examine the simplest aspects of the social control of crime.

It must mean something that the only Son of God was a criminal defendant, and that his experiences are echoed in our modern laws, customs, and habits. If God intends that we learn from the stories of Jesus, then we must learn, too, from the people and the society that tried, convicted, imprisoned, tortured, and executed Jesus.

CHAPTER TWO

THE INVESTIGATION AND INCULPATORY STATEMENTS

"Woe to you lawyers! For you have taken away the key of knowledge; you did not enter yourselves, and you hindered those who were entering." When he went outside, the scribes and the Pharisees began to be very hostile toward him and to cross-examine him about many things, lying in wait for him, to catch him in something he might say. —Luke 11:52-54

In my office is a blown-up photograph of a large, angry man approaching a car. The photograph was taken by FBI agents sitting in that car, and it still bears an exhibit sticker from the trial of that large, angry man, whose name is Beck Wooten.

Wooten operated one of the largest fencing operations in Michigan, buying stolen auto parts from thieves and selling them to wholesalers. In the late 1990s, car theft and break-ins spiked in southeastern Michigan, and I hoped to stop that trend by locking up the fences and denying the thieves a market for their goods. To me, it was personal; three times thieves had broken into my car to steal the radio. In my plan for retribution, target number one was Beck Wooten.

Heading our investigation was FBI Special Agent John Ryan, an affable, intelligent man with thick glasses, an engineering degree, and a wonderfully creative mind. As we took on the case, some of our colleagues were discouraging, telling us that such cases were very hard to prove. The problem, we were told, was proving the element of knowledge—that is, showing a jury beyond a reasonable doubt that Wooten knew that what he was buying was stolen. The problem was compounded by the fact that Wooten usually got signed statements from his "vendors" saying that the radios, tires, and air bags they had to sell were not stolen.

It is a difficult thing to prove what is in someone's mind. There are really only two ways to prove a person's state of mind (such as knowledge or intent). First, a prosecutor can make a circumstantial case based on observable facts that would seem to reflect such a state of mind. For example, in the Wooten case, the bare fact that the same indigent individuals came to him day after day with the same sets of goods would seem to inform him that those goods were stolen.

The problem with circumstantial proofs is that they are, well, circumstantial. The prosecutor must ask a jury to infer what the person was thinking, and the defense attorney often will be able to show equally plausible and innocent explanations. For example, the indigents selling car parts to a fence could be working for a legitimate salvage operation.

The second option is the only direct form of evidence showing a state of mind: inculpatory statements. Inculpatory statements are those made by the target, in either oral or written form, which show that he knows or intends something. For example, if a drug dealer tells an undercover agent that he is selling "the best coke in town," then those words will serve as direct evidence that he knew what he was selling was cocaine and not a bag of sugar or baking soda.

Inculpatory statements are extremely valuable to the government in a prosecution that involves a state of mind such as knowledge or intent because there is no substitute for simple evidence showing that the defendant *stated* what he knew or intended. The high value of these statements as evidence explains why investigators take such risks and make commitments of time to get them. It is to get such inculpatory statements that police officers risk their lives to go undercover as drug addicts or take a blood oath and join a gang.

John Ryan, instead of going undercover, relied on his intelligence to get the direct evidence we needed. Borrowing a page from classic drug investigations, where state of mind is often a difficult element to prove, Special Agent Ryan wrote a fifty-page affidavit seeking to place a wiretap on Beck Wooten's phone and an electronic bug in his office. We then got court approval and set up a listening station with FBI agents overseeing the recordings of conversations. The payoff was huge. At trial we were able to put before the jury the recording of a phone call that Wooten made to a customer in California, in which he referred to the air bags he had to sell as "steals." Wooten was locked up, his business was forfeited, and auto break-ins declined more than 70 percent in the area. All of that was possible only because we were able to catch Wooten making an inculpatory statement.

Times haven't changed much. Like me in the Wooten case, Jesus' investigators were highly motivated. Jesus was a direct threat to them and traveled the countryside denouncing them in the harshest terms, calling them a corrupt "brood of vipers" (Matt 23:33).

To the prosecutor, what is intriguing is the form of investigation that the religious authorities chose once they identified their target. Subsequent chapters will address two fascinating aspects of that investigation: the use of a paid informant, and the strategic arrest of the target, both of which were totally consistent with modern use of those techniques. Here, we will focus on another aspect of that investigation—the efforts to get the target to make an inculpatory statement, a statement that would be valuable for precisely the same reason as that million-dollar tape in which Beck Wooten uttered the word *steals*.

First, however, let us return to the motivation of the investigators. Jesus' ministry was not sympathetic to the religious authorities of the time. He often railed against them in his sermons, singling them out as the worst sort of hypocrites: "They devour widows' houses and for the sake of appearance say long prayers. They will receive the greater condemnation" (Mark 12:40).

Perhaps worse, he compared the Pharisees unfavorably to tax collectors. In Luke 18, he told of two men who went to the temple to pray. The first was a Pharisee, who prayed, "God, I thank you that I am not like other people: thieves, rogues, adulterers, or even like this tax collector." The second was the very tax collector that the Pharisee condemned. Unlike the self-congratulatory Pharisee, the tax collector beat his chest and pleaded simply, "God, be merciful to me, a sinner!" (vv. 11, 13). In viewing those two, Jesus concluded that the tax collector, rather than the religious leader, was to be exalted.

At other times, Jesus was even blunter in his assessment of those who would become his prosecutors. He told them that they crossed "sea and land to make a single convert" and made "the new convert twice as much a child of hell" as themselves (Matt 23:15), and that they were "like whitewashed tombs, which on the outside look beautiful, but inside they are full of the bones of the dead and of all kinds of filth" (Matt 23:27). Not only did he condemn them, but he did so in front of crowds of people, the very people who were expected to tithe to and follow those same religious leaders.

The threat felt by the leaders was to their very legitimacy and livelihood, not to something as mundane as a car radio. Jesus clearly did not fear the authorities, but they had reason to fear Jesus and the social changes he sought. Unmistakably, they started an investigation and tried to trick Jesus into making the inculpatory statement that would make their job easy.

In seeking such an inculpatory statement, the religious leaders seemed to want Jesus to utter something so contrary to civil or church law that it would be almost indefensible. After all, state of mind was at the heart of the crimes with which Christ was ultimately accused—*intent* to destroy the temple and *belief* that he was the Son of God—and no evidence would be as good as an admission from the defendant that he had that intent or belief. The Bible chronicles several of their attempts to tease out such a statement.

The Pharisees were not alone in trying to trap Jesus. Mark 12:13 makes clear that the interrogators included "Herodians." Thus, the religious authorities seemed to have been joined in their endeavor by the more secular agents of Herod. As with so many other parts of the story, the use of investigators from multiple authorities working together exists now as it did then. Today, we call such groupings a task force, and thousands of them, formal and informal, have been involved in investigations of crimes in the United States. In the Beck Wooten case, for example, Special Agent Ryan and I worked closely with officers from the city of Detroit, who had a very different kind of expertise, base of knowledge, and authority than we did. A target who was questioned by both Special Agent Ryan and a seasoned lieutenant of the Detroit police department was facing a nearly seamless wall of knowledge regarding the law and the streets.

The interrogations of Jesus took many forms, though each was a nearly transparent attempt to trick him into saying something that would anger the civil authorities or constitute a serious violation of church doctrine. For example, in the presence of the Herodians, they put before Jesus a question designed to get him in trouble with the Romans, given his history of antiauthoritarian actions: "Is it lawful to pay taxes to the emperor, or not?" (Mark 12:14).

Jesus both recognized the question as a trap and proceeded to answer it. "Why are you putting me to the test?" he asked them, before telling them to "bring me a denarius and let me see it" (Mark 12:15). Famously, he asked the interrogators whose head was depicted on the coin. It was the emperor's, of course, as they had to acknowledge. Then Jesus commanded, "Give to the emperor the things that are the emperor's, and to God the things that are God's" (Mark 12:17).

As a postscript to the story, Mark added that the interrogators "were utterly amazed at him" (Mark 12:17). Amazed? Probably, they were amazed not by the antimaterialism of the teaching (money is not of God), but by the ability of the target to simultaneously evade the trap by recognizing the need to pay taxes while remaining true to his theology.

Immediately following Mark's description of the tax-question trap is the tale of another group of church leaders attempting to draw an inculpatory statement out of Jesus. The Sadducees, a distinct and powerful group that was separate from and often at odds with the Pharisees, cornered him. While the Pharisees tried to trick Jesus into a conflict with the Romans, the Sadducees tried to create a conflict between Jesus' teaching that there is an afterlife and the teachings of Moses.

Really, it was a riddle that the Sadducees put before Jesus. They first reminded Jesus that Moses had commanded that if a man died childless, the widow was to then marry the dead man's brother. The

Sadducees stretched this commandment out to ridiculous lengths, describing a family with seven brothers who died one by one without children, as the first brother's wife became the wife to each of them in turn. Having spun this hypothetical, they asked Jesus which of the seven husbands the woman would be with at the time of the resurrection, when the dead will rise (Mark 12:18-23).

Once again, Jesus escaped the net of inculpation without giving away his principles. They tried to trap him between the law of Moses' implication that there is no afterlife and his own teachings that there is one; he escaped by teaching that they misunderstood what such an afterlife would be: "Is not this the reason you are wrong, that you know neither the scriptures nor the power of God? For when they rise from the dead, they neither marry nor are given in marriage, but are like angels in heaven" (Mark 12:24-25).

Having defeated the snares of the Pharisees and the Sadducees, Jesus was challenged next by another group that wielded great power within the church and society—the scribes. This group included both Pharisees and Sadducees, who were defined by their tasks more than anything else. They were literate and made copies of key manuscripts, including the law. They also were called on to interpret the law, and they spoke publicly about the positions they took. It was probably the scribes who constituted the "lawyers" that Jesus condemned at the start of Luke 11:52, quoted at the beginning of this chapter.

After Jesus finished speaking with the Sadducees, Mark reported that a single scribe approached Jesus and asked what appeared to be a simple question: "Which commandment is the first of all?" (Mark 12:28).

It was hardly a simple question. Remember that the scribe had the job of writing down the commandments found in the Old Testament, which run into the thousands and even today provide the grist for innumerable arguments regarding their relative value. The scribe wanted to join in the game of trapping Jesus into speaking contrary to the law of the faith, which had grown hopelessly complex. Like politicians everywhere, the scribe hoped that Jesus would either pick one, and thus denigrate the others, or say that all were important and back away from the task.

As he did with the Pharisees and the Sadducees, Jesus deftly parried the question of the scribe without either exposing himself to condemnation or giving up his principles. He answered quite directly: "The first is, 'Hear, O Israel: the Lord our God, the Lord is one; you shall love the Lord your God with all your heart, and with all your soul, and with all your mind, and with all your strength'" (Mark 12:29-30).

Unlike the Pharisees and the Sadducees, the scribe acknowledged that Jesus spoke wisely, saying, "You are right, Teacher" (Mark 12:32).

Having almost simultaneously turned away the traps of the Pharisees, the Sadducees, and a scribe, Jesus apparently went on to prove that they could have done even better in the area of tricky questions. Among the same crowd that witnessed the other challenges, Jesus asked himself a hopelessly tricky question: "How can the scribes say that the Messiah is the son of David?" (Mark 12:35). Given that he held himself out as the Messiah, this question seemed to go to the heart of what could easily become an inculpatory statement of blasphemy (specifically, the claim of being God). But even in response to his own question, Jesus did not inculpate himself, saying only that "David himself calls [the Messiah] Lord; so how can he be his son?" (Mark 12:37). This answer neither provided the fodder for a charge of blasphemy nor diverged from Jesus' teachings. Rather, it seems fairly inscrutable to the modern ear.

While it is hard for a layperson such as myself to sort out the full theological meaning of Jesus' response to his own question, the crowd present that day seemed to understand the larger drama. Mark reported that the "large crowd was listening to him with delight" (Mark 12:37). Of course the crowd did! Imagine the scene with yourself in that crowd—three different types of authority figures came to question and trap Jesus, and he masterfully avoided their traps while staying consistent with his teaching. Finally, the snares evaded, he took on an additional question that he posed himself and answered such as not to implicate himself. Who would not listen in delight?

In a separate incident, "the chief priests and the elders of the people" stopped Jesus (Matt 21:23). Clearly, they too wanted to trick him into making a claim that would sound like blasphemy. As he was about to teach, they asked him, "By what authority are you doing these things, and who gave you this authority?" (Matt 21:23). The answer, it would seem (and the chief priests probably hoped), would be that Jesus taught by the authority of God.

But once again, Jesus answered honestly while refusing to hand the authorities the rope with which to hang him. Instead, he answered the question with another question: "Did the baptism of John come from heaven, or was it of human origin?" (Matt 21:25). This response flummoxed the chief priests, who knew that if they said John's authority came from God, it would undermine their treatment of John, and if they said John's authority came from human beings, they would lose the support of the crowd (Matt 21:25-26). In the end, they responded, "We do not know" (Matt 21:27), and the situation was defused.

Interestingly, at each step Jesus could easily have given the authorities what they would have considered an inculpatory answer, stating that he was the Son of God or at least admitting that God was the source of his authority. Instead, he made the authorities work for this information from other sources, a choice that made later proceedings much more difficult.

Of course, things might have been different had the religious authorities had the ability to place an electronic bug among Jesus and his disciples rather than try to trick him into following his theology into a trap. Technology aside, however, the goal of these techniques is the same: to gather direct evidence in the form of a spoken or written statement of what a person is thinking so that the state of mind can be conclusively proved at trial. Without that direct evidence, a trial can be a tangled, confusing mess dependent on the observations of often-unreliable witnesses and the fierce arguments of prosecutors. That was precisely, as we will see, what the trial of Christ ultimately became.

CHAPTER THREE

THE USE OF A PAID INFORMANT

Then one of the twelve, who was called Judas Iscariot, went to the chief priests and said, "What will you give me if I betray him to you?" They paid him thirty pieces of silver. And from that moment he began to look for an opportunity to betray him.

—Matthew 26:14-16

A few years ago, a shop owner in Baltimore made a crudely filmed DVD he called *Stop Snitching* and sold it in his store for ten dollars. Helped in part by the fact that the video included NBA star Carmelo Anthony, it became an underground hit and spawned a cottage industry of other "Stop Snitching" products, including T-shirts, which became commonplace in some neighborhoods.

Because the point of the "Stop Snitching" campaign was to urge people not to provide information to the government about the criminal activities of others, the government was, of course, outraged. Boston's Mayor Thomas M. Menino even threatened to go to every store selling the shirts and take them off the shelves.[1] The FBI in Philadelphia, specifically in response to "Stop Snitching" shirts appearing around the city (and even in courtrooms), started a reeducation program it called "Step Up, Speak Up."

Some regarded the "Stop Snitching" campaign as backlash against a system of informants that had too large a role in criminal investigations and prosecutions. As Alexandra Natapoff wrote in *Slate*, "Stop Snitching" was just one

> symptom of a more insidious reality that has largely escaped public notice: For the last 20 years, state and federal governments have been creating criminal snitches and setting them loose in poor, high crime neighborhoods. The backlash against snitches embodies a growing national recognition that snitching is dangerous public policy—producing bad information, endangering innocent people, letting dangerous criminals off the hook, compromising the integrity of police work, and inciting violence and distrust in socially vulnerable neighborhoods.[2]

Both sides of this contemporary debate have a point. On the one hand, confidential informants are probably overused, primarily because they are cheap and efficient, if not necessarily reliable. On the other hand, particularly in the realm of narcotics investigations, they are often necessary if the structure and actions of the criminals are to be detected and stopped.

At the same time that the legal world fussed over the import of the "Stop Snitching" campaign, the most famous snitch in history, Judas Iscariot, came into public view with the publication of the ancient gnostic *Gospel of Judas*. That text, lost for centuries in places as varied as the sands of Egypt and a safe-deposit box at a Citibank branch in Hicksville, New York, puts a more positive spin on Judas's actions, but does not relieve him of the role that history assigns him—that of informer.[3]

To set Judas within the context of the modern snitch, it is helpful to understand the two basic types of informants: confidential informants (sometimes called CI's) and cooperating defendants. Though some snitches fit both descriptions, most are in one category or the other.

The first type is the confidential informant. Most confidential informants are involved on the fringes of low-level criminal activities and provide information on a regular basis to a police officer or agent about potential targets, information that will serve as the basis for requesting search warrants and locating those who have been charged so they may be arrested. The primary motivation for confidential informants is usually to get paid. Some are able to live very well, and "superstars" can make more than one hundred thousand dollars in high-profile cases.[4]

Aside from working for pay, confidential informants rarely testify at trials. To make such a public appearance would ruin their secret on the street and make them useless as sources. For that reason, confidential informants are usually (but not always) used in roles where they will not be exposed to public view. For example, one primary use of confidential informants is to be the basis for obtaining a search warrant. Say that you are a prosecutor, and you have received a tip that a methamphetamine lab is operating in your area. You cannot prosecute on that tip, and you need to generate further evidence. To do so, you want to search the home where the lab is located and seize the meth-making equipment. In order to obtain a warrant, you need reliable information that meth is made and sold from that location. Typically, an officer will unlock this puzzle by sending a confidential informant to buy methamphetamines and observe what is in the house. If he goes in and sees a meth lab, a search warrant application will be drawn up relying on his information, claiming prior good experiences with this CI, and protecting the identity of that informant with a coded number. To the main dealers, the confidential informant will be just another neighborhood drug addict who passed through, and he will be able to utilize this trick again and again.

Confidential informants, of course, create problems. Chief among those problems is that they can be involved in precisely the crime that the police are using the informants to investigate. For example, it isn't uncommon to discover that the confidential informant sent in to bust up the meth operation is operating his own factory down the block, subsidized by what he is paid by the government. As an added benefit, the informant gets to eliminate any competition.

Oversight on confidential informants is particularly difficult, in part because their unseen role is not clear to the prosecutor. The confidential informant communicates and reports to the agent or officer, who then takes a case to the prosecutor once it is developed. Very often, by the time an agent takes a file to the prosecutor for review, the entire role of the informant has been completed. As a federal prosecutor, I rarely was aware of a confidential informant's identity. Not once do I remember meeting such informants, other than those whom we planned to call as witnesses. Unfortunately, the person with the most legal training and experience on the side of the investigators, the prosecutor, often plays no role in the over-sight of ongoing confidential informants working the street for information.

In September 2005, the inspector general of the FBI released a report finding that 87 percent of the confidential informant files examined revealed a violation of FBI rules.[5] If they are honest, agents and police officers will describe the process of supervising confidential informants as akin to herding cats; their nature is to wander off and do what they want. Then uncomfortable situations arise when confidential informants are arrested for wrongdoing and look to their "client" officers for assistance.

The second type of snitch is the cooperating defendant. Generally, the cooperating defendant is swept up with other members of a conspiracy and then decides to testify against the other members of the group. Sometimes, as with Judas, a cooperating defendant will volunteer information prior to the government's arrests.

Cooperating defendants differ from confidential informants in several ways. First, cooperating defendants generally seek not money, but freedom from prosecution. Second, cooperating defendants almost always have direct contact with the prosecutor and often have lawyers of their own. Finally, cooperating defendants are most often useful only in a single case and are not kept on a continuing retainer. Unlike confidential informants who want to keep their identity secret, cooperating defendants can be useful to the prosecution as trial witnesses, and this often is their primary role.

With both confidential informants and cooperating defendants, despite their differences, the major danger to justice stems from their eagerness to help the government. They know that if they are to get the benefit they seek (cash or a break on their own cases), the government must be pleased with what they say. Because of this strong incentive, some commentators have condemned the practice as an incentive to perjury.[6]

Judas probably better fit the profile of the confidential informant than the cooperating defendant since it seemed the authorities were primarily after Jesus alone, and Judas was not one of their targets. Either way, if eagerness is the root of the problem when it comes to cooperators and informants, how does this relate to Judas? The Gospels, and even the newly found *Gospel of Judas*, answer that question by describing a Judas who was the epitome of eagerness and motivation (though they differ on what that motivation was). He was motivated enough that he provided his information to the authorities despite Jesus' warning that if he was given over to the chief priests, he would be killed (Matt 17:22-23). Judas's eagerness is so repellent that two millennia later his name is taken as an insult, while Peter (who committed a similar but less serious sin when he denied Jesus three times) is revered.[7]

We know that Judas was eager because he proactively sought out those who wanted to trap and destroy Jesus. Each of the four Gospels reports that it was Judas who went to the chief priests to provide information (Matt 26:14; Mark 14:10; Luke 22:4; John 18:3). Nor is it likely that Judas went to the authorities even in response to a general request for information. As theologian Raymond Brown noted, the authorities probably did not seek out such aid because they had a "desire to avoid a riot meant that they could not have sought help publicly."[8]

It is settled that Judas was motivated to turn in Jesus, leaving open the question of his motivation. On this point, there are multiple theories.

The *Gospel of Judas* suggests that Judas was actually one of Jesus' favorites and was assigned the task of going to the authorities so that Jesus could meet his fate as it was prophesied. That document, which has been partially recovered, describes a Jesus Christ who often laughed and seemed to enjoy his time with his apostles, even as he was frustrated by how little they understood. There, Jesus told

Judas that "you will exceed all of them. For you will sacrifice the man that clothes me."[9] The modern editors of that gospel interpret this (within the theology of that gnostic gospel) to mean that "Judas is instructed by Jesus to help him by sacrificing the fleshly body that clothes or bears the true spiritual self of Jesus."[10] From that somewhat tenuous source, at least, Judas's motivation was Christ's request and flattery.

That, of course, is not the traditional view of Judas's motivation. The traditional Gospels portray Judas as someone strongly motivated by money, a theme that developed well before his decision to take the thirty silver coins.

John 12 describes Judas as the keeper of the purse for the apostles, the one who maintained the finances for the group of thirteen. Given that the group included at least two former tax collectors (Levi and Matthew), it seems odd that Judas received the task, and it could well be that he sought it out, establishing a money nexus that defined his relationship with Jesus from the start to the last.

One would imagine that controlling the money for so many men would be a complex task at times. The role of purse keeper would also make Judas a great informant. Investigators know that if you are to break down how a criminal organization is structured, the best way is to follow the money. The flow of cash tells an investigator much of what she needs to know: who is most important in an organization (the money ends up in his or her hands), who is involved, how large an organization it is, when the group commits crimes, and how successful the group is at its chosen course. The money doesn't lie; therefore, the person who controls the money is very often the one with the best information. Sometimes the purse keeper is the only one in the organization who fully understands its scope and effects, and may be the only conspirator who knows the names of all those involved.

Thus, Judas would have been a valuable informant, but his access to money is not the story we are after here as we look to his motivations. His actions in holding the purse revealed that motivation: a certain heartless greed. In talking about Judas's role as the bank for the apostles, John went beyond describing Judas as the apostolic comptroller; he stated that Judas "was a thief; he kept the common purse and used to steal what was put into it" (John 12:6). Because the apostles and Jesus relied on the generosity of others, the purse may have been filled with the donations of poor persons. At least according to John, Judas was someone so motivated by greed that he would steal from the common funds given by their supporters.

Judas's focus on cash brought him into conflict with Jesus well before he became an informant. Six days before the Passover that framed his death, Jesus went to visit the home of Lazarus, whom he had raised from the dead. One would imagine that Lazarus's family would have been quite grateful to Jesus, and it appears that they were. During the evening, Lazarus's sister, Mary, took expensive perfume and used it to anoint Jesus' feet, which (in a striking visual image of humility) she then wiped clean with her hair (John 12:1-3).

Jesus allowed her to do that. He was chastised, though, by Judas, the keeper of the purse, who said, "Why was this perfume not sold for three hundred denarii and the money given to the poor?" In response, Jesus told Judas to "leave her alone," and he added that "you always have the poor with you, but you do not always have me" (John 12:5-8).

It is, in context of what is to happen the following week, a chilling scene and could be part of the reason that Judas decided to betray his leader. This tale of money, Judas, and the death of Jesus foreshadows the conflicts within many criminal gangs that lead a member to become an informant. The cooperator often feels that he or she has been humiliated or misunderstood by the leader or leaders, and that this humiliation, such as being publicly upbraided, cut the ties of trust. Like many modern snitches, this ancient one may well have acted out of resentment, having been embarrassed by Jesus at dinner.

It would seem, also, that Jesus probably did not value the task of the holder of the purse very highly, given his consistent refusal to use his talents to enrich himself. This frugality extended to Jesus' expectations for the apostles. In sending them out to "proclaim the good news," he instructed them specifically not to receive payment, not to take money with them, and not to carry a bag with posses-sions. They were further forbidden from carrying a second tunic, and were told to stay with those who would have them (Matt 10:5-11). In a group that so devalued wealth, what would the status of the purse holder be? Simple human emotions and resentment, com-bined with greed, seem to easily explain Judas's tragic choice and track the motivations of many modern informants.

Once he decided to become an informant, how helpful was Judas? We know at the least that he gave the authorities the very important tip about Jesus' location, something that informants often do. It could be that he gave them additional information as well, such as the identities of the others associated with Jesus and the activities of the group. He might even have described the state-ments that led to the charges of blasphemy and plotting to destroy the temple; we just don't know. Even in the gnostic *Gospel of Judas*, the information he provided is vague, relating only that when meeting with the high priests, he "answered them as they wished."[11]

That is not to say that identifying the physical location of Jesus was inconsequential to the arresting authorities. As Raymond Brown points out, the authorities faced several challenges in locat-ing Jesus that night: Jerusalem was swollen with crowds for the feast days; Jesus usually stayed outside the city walls, expanding the area that would have to be searched; Jesus had not been in Jerusalem long enough to establish a firm residence; and Jesus had (according to John) eluded arrest in the city by hiding himself.[12] The help that Judas provided in finding a man in that setting certainly benefited those making the arrest and minimized the risks associated with a wide-ranging or door-to-door search at the time of the feast. Given the risks, even if that was the only information Judas provided, he probably was a bargain at the rate of just one-tenth the value of the perfume poured on Jesus' feet.[13]

The betrayal itself was a drama worthy of the act's importance. As described by Matthew, Judas went with those making the arrest, and they arrived as Jesus was trying to keep some of his other followers awake. Judas accompanied the authorities, who were carrying swords and clubs. He told them, "The one I will kiss is the man; arrest him" (Matt 26:47-48). Judas approached Jesus, greeted him, and kissed him, and his role was over.

And what of that kiss? It seems an odd form of identification, but it had the advantage of providing certainty among a crowd. It is a compelling image as well. We might imagine that this part, at least, is not connected to modern practice, and I certainly haven't heard of this being done in a recent case. Yet the image is familiar in our modern media. The paradigm of criminality in the United States is the Mafia, and the depictions of those criminals in a television show like *The Sopranos* and a movie such as *The Godfather* include, always, the iconic mobster greeting: the kiss. To the mobsters, as they are portrayed in the media, the platonic kiss of men is a sign of a bond. Upon meeting a boss, the underling delivers a kiss. When someone is released from prison, he is greeted with a kiss as well.

As our society becomes steadily less literate in understanding the Bible and more culturally literate in our knowledge of mass entertainment, it could be that the kiss a *Sopranos* character gives to mob boss Tony Soprano while wearing a wire is better known than the betraying kiss of Judas, even as it echoes that ancient signal.

It seems that the informants, like the poor, will always be with us, for good or bad. The tale of Judas is compelling for the same reason "Stop Snitching" became the focus of the FBI: informants play a central role not only in the everyday machinations of criminal law, but also in the morality tales that inform and challenge our ideas and beliefs about loyalty, virtue, duty, and betrayal.

CHAPTER FOUR

STRATEGIC ARREST

He came and found them sleeping; and he said to Peter, "Simon, are you asleep? Could you not keep awake one hour? Keep awake and pray that you may not come into the time of trial; the spirit indeed is willing, but the flesh is weak." And again he went and prayed, saying the same words. And once more he came and found them sleeping, for their eyes were very heavy; and they did not know what to say to him. He came a third time and said to them, "Are you still sleeping and taking your rest? Enough! The hour has come; the Son of Man is betrayed into the hands of sinners. Get up, let us be going. See, my betrayer is at hand."

Immediately, while he was still speaking, Judas, one of the twelve, arrived; and with him there was a crowd with swords and clubs, from the chief priests, the scribes, and the elders.

—Mark 14:37-43

Hidden at Gethsemane, knowing that he was being pursued by the authorities and suspecting that one of his inner circle was betraying him, the Jesus described in Mark 14 seemed a wary and worried fugitive, struggling to keep his supporters awake.

Two modern aspects mark the arrest of Jesus: first, the authorities arrived with overwhelming force, and second, the arrest was made when those authorities expected Jesus and his followers to be asleep. There is no mystical connection between these events and modern practice; rather, both factors are commonsense procedures designed to give a strategic advantage to the authorities over a fugitive. For example, the authorities chose the hours of darkness for the same reason that arrests today are often in the early morning hours; the target and his supporters would be asleep and easy to apprehend. The Bible expressly describes that Jesus' arresters, like those of today, "were looking for a way to arrest Jesus by stealth" (Mark 14:1), and chose not to arrest him during the Passover festival because that would risk facing his angry (and wide-awake) supporters.

Anyone who doubts that these tactics continue into the present day can, with some sense of irony, consider the case of Jesus' spiritual opposite, the violent and radical Sheik Omar Abdel Rahman.

Rahman was at the center of the group that planted a bomb in the World Trade Center in 1993, and he issued a religious order that his followers blow up the Lincoln and Holland tunnels in New York City and attack American military bases. Rahman, a blind Egyptian cleric who held a powerful influence over his followers, relied on an inner circle of confidants to carry out his plans and communicate with the larger world. In his speeches, he preached that the government of the United States was evil and need not be respected or obeyed.[1]

Eventually, the federal government procured the help of an informant, Emad Salem, who worked within Rahman's trusted inner circle. Even though Rahman suspected that one of his followers would betray him, Salem apparently was able to provide the government with the information it needed, including the location of a safe house where Rahman was hiding with eight of his followers. With the aid of that informant, FBI agents raided the safe house at 2:00 a.m., June 24, 1993, presumably as the defendants were sleeping.[2]

As a prosecutor working with agents from several federal and state agencies, I heard stories of various raids of safe houses, drug houses, and storehouses. There was a certain similarity to the stories, given that the same procedures were usually followed. Through hearing these conversations and observing a few raids, I realized the importance of these procedures. Overwhelming force and the element of surprise ensure the safety of the arresting officers and allow a "clean" arrest.

The element of surprise was relatively easy for us on the side of law enforcement to produce, provided that we did not mind getting up very early in the morning. In narcotics and firearm cases, a search and arrest would often be executed at 6:00 a.m. when the targets and their accomplices and/or families were likely to be asleep. As the chief priests recognized, doing this avoided the resistance that one would expect if the residents were awake, and the house was easier to approach without being detected. It also was easier to gather evidence, since sleeping people would not be able to dispose of contraband when the police knocked on the door and announced their presence.

Other strategic motives directed arrests at other times. For example, if a defendant did not pose a threat to the arresting party, the arrest could be made publicly to heighten the humiliation of the defendant and, in turn, the deterrent value of the arrest. When he was the United States attorney for the Southern District of New York, Rudolph Giuliani sought to deter other criminals by making arrests as public as possible. Financial traders accused of crimes were arrested at their places of work, maximizing their shame as they were led out of their offices in handcuffs past stunned and staring coworkers.[3] When the person being arrested is an ashen-faced stockbroker, the chance of violence is greatly reduced, unlike the situation the FBI faced in arresting Sheik Rahman.

The second strategic pattern followed in police raids is the use of overwhelming force. A single officer rarely, if ever, raids a home to make an arrest or search. Rather, a heavily armed team performs the task in order to quickly overwhelm whoever might be in the house. Each member of the team, often a task force comprising officers and agents from different jurisdictions, has a specialized job. These jobs are assigned at a staging meeting, usually held near the target location but not within eyesight of the target. For example, people are designated to use a battering ram to break down a locked door; to enter the house first and evaluate the situation, including the presence of people or dogs; to knock and announce the entry; and to identify, incapacitate, and arrest the target.

Witnessing a dynamic entry into a home or safe house is a memorable event. The entry occurs with striking speed, again to enable the officers to catch the targets unaware and unable to mount a defense. As the officers approach the building, they are as quiet as possible. Some of them fan out to guard possible exits from the building, including back doors and side windows. The arrest begins with a knock and a shout by the officer standing at the door. Quickly, he or she steps away, and two or more officers with a ram break down the door. What happens next is a cacophony—the officers shouting, "Get down! Get down!" to anyone they encounter, a dog barking, the targets yelling as they are taken down. Inside the house, the point man is followed by several others with guns drawn. If they encounter a dog that appears menacing, it often is shot. When officers find individuals in the house, whether or not they are targets of the investigation, they are forced to lie down on the floor, frisked, and usually handcuffed. The shouting and drawn weapons are necessary and intentional; the officers hope that the show of force will discourage any violent reaction by the residents of the house.

These procedures are not simple technicalities. The failure to arrest cleanly can and does result in physical injury and death for law enforcement personnel and for those who are targeted for arrest. A particularly tragic example was the attempt to arrest David Koresh, the leader of the Branch Davidians, on February 28, 1993. The Branch Davidians, originally an offshoot of the Seventh-day Adventist Church, had become a cult of personality around Koresh. Taking the group of more than one hundred followers in a dangerous direction, Koresh instructed his flock to amass weapons and to view the federal government, and in particular the Bureau of Alcohol, Tobacco, and Firearms (ATF), as an evil "beast."[4]

In executing the warrant against Koresh, the ATF failed both to bring overwhelming force and to time the raid to avoid armed conflict. Although the ATF brought several agents to the scene in two cattle trailers, they faced a group of more than one hundred people in a fortified compound, armed with automatic weapons. The agency could have asked for help from other federal or local agencies, but it appears that none was requested and received, and they went in alone.

Their timing was also unfortunate. Instead of conducting the raid at night, they mounted the raid in the heat of the day. As the Fifth Circuit Court of Appeals described it, the result was tragic:

> The ATF decided to execute the search and arrest warrant on February 28, 1993, but as it was to learn, the element of surprise had been lost. Around 8:00 a.m., an undercover ATF agent, Roberto Rodriguez, visited the Davidian compound and spoke with Koresh. During the conversation, Koresh took a phone call. When he returned, a visibly shaken Koresh told Rodriguez, "Robert, neither the AFT or National Guard will ever get me. They got me once, they'll never get me again." Koresh then walked over to the windows and looked toward the farmhouse used by the undercover ATF agents. He turned to Rodriguez and said, "They're coming, Robert. The time has come." Rodriguez left the compound around 9:00 a.m. and advised the ATF that Koresh had learned of the raid at least forty-five minutes earlier.
>
> The ATF decided to proceed with the arrest and search warrants. The plan quickly went awry. The helicopters did not arrive until after the ATF agents had begun unloading from the cattle trailers. As the agents unloaded, gunfire erupted from the compound, and the agents returned fire. In the ensuing gun battle, four agents and three Davidians were killed. Twenty-two ATF agents and four Davidians were wounded.[5]

After this botched raid, the FBI took over and besieged the complex for fifty-one days. That siege ended with the second, even more tragic raid on the compound in which fire and bullets consumed most of the Davidians, including David Koresh.

Having looked in the present day to the arrests of two religious leaders who chose violence, let us now look back to the arrest of Jesus, who did not.

From what Mark describes, it certainly seems that the authorities entered the hiding place at Gethsemane with overwhelming force. The "crowd with swords and clubs" (Mark 14:43) brings to mind the helmeted, rifle-carrying agents who effect arrests today. As theologian Raymond Brown noted, swords were, at that time, military weapons, the equivalent of today's military rifles.[6] Because they came bearing such weapons, Brown seems to feel that the arresters were an organized party, and that the view that they were nothing more than rabble or a mob is an "overinterpretation."[7]

The Gospel of John is perhaps even more graphic than Mark's version in profiling those making the arrest as "a detachment of soldiers together with police from the chief priests and the Pharisees, and they came there with lanterns and torches and weapons" (John 18:3). John's description brings forth a new aspect of the arrest—a task force was involved, including both the police from the religious authorities and soldiers from the Roman-controlled military. Raymond Brown (who had the language skills and training to understand the original text in ways that I cannot) holds that what John describes as "police" and "soldiers" were distinct Jewish and Roman members of that task force because John "clearly distinguishes these troops, for whom he uses technical Roman terminology, from the attendants supplied by 'chief priests and the Pharisees.'"[8] While these Roman troops were probably not crack legionnaires or even ethnic Romans, they were at the least Roman recruits from the Syro-Palestinian area.[9] The soldiers were there not under the command of religious authorities, either, but reporting to their own Roman officer (John 18:12), who would have held the rank of military tribune.[10]

In the setting of a problematic arrest, task forces provide distinct advantages. First, they allow for a larger arresting party, providing the overwhelming force necessary when the target is protected by a group of supporters. Second, they allow for a range of expertise and experience. Third (and especially significant in this context), they allow for easier prosecution through multiple jurisdictions, either independently or through cooperation.

The element of surprise was also present in the arrest of Jesus, in that the task force made the conscious decision to arrest at night rather than when Jesus was walking in the city during the Passover festival. As he was arrested, Jesus noted that fact, asking the soldiers, "Have you come out with swords and clubs as if I were a bandit? When I was with you day after day in the temple, you did not lay hands on me. But this is your hour, and the power of darkness!"

(Luke 22:52-53). He had, of course, guessed correctly that they did not want to wrangle with his supporters in public (Mark 14:2). Little has changed about the power of darkness.

Despite the use of overwhelming force and the element of surprise, the scene at Gethsemane was chaotic. As described in the next chapter, Peter sliced off the ear of one of the arresting party (John 18:10), and one can only imagine the reaction of the others among the Twelve when Judas arrived at the head of the group of soldiers and police (Luke 22:47).

The mayhem at the scene extended beyond the violence of Peter. For example, Mark reports that at the time of the arrest, one of those accompanying Jesus was a young man "wearing nothing but a linen cloth. They caught hold of him, but he left the linen cloth and ran off naked" (Mark 14:51-52). Apparently, though, he had nothing to fear; the authorities arrested and took away only Jesus. The others were left to scatter on their own, and the Bible reports that they "deserted him and fled" (Mark 14:50).

There is something subtle and powerful about an arrest. At its most fundamental level, it is at the exact moment of arrest that the state takes the defendant's body, beginning the thorough process of physical control that marks the criminal justice system. There is no theory to it, no legal principle that anyone is thinking about as the battering ram is unloaded from a van. Rather, it is a raw and violent exercise of power by the state over someone whose physical freedom has been judged dangerous. It is often a loud, dramatic, contentious moment, and the procedures I have described above, and the planning of the police, are intended to further the advantages of the authorities in this crucial task.

As much as there are similarities between the arrest of Jesus and the arrest of Sheik Rahman or the attempted arrest of David Koresh, there is also a crucial difference for the Christian. In the end, Jesus Christ stopped the efforts of his followers and said, "Let the scriptures be fulfilled" (Mark 14:49), and so they were.

CHAPTER FIVE

THE MAIMING OF THE SLAVE AND THE ROLE OF POWER

When those who were around him saw what was coming, they asked, "Lord, should we strike with the sword?" Then one of them struck the slave of the high priest and cut off his right ear. But Jesus said, "No more of this!" And he touched his ear and healed him.
—Luke 22:49-51

It was not easy to arrest Jesus. He was hiding, surrounded by his supporters, some of whom apparently were armed. There was a strong history of antagonism between the arresting party and the targets, and the targets suspected that an arrest was coming. Perhaps predictably, the targets reacted to the encounter with violence, attacking the arresters. Only at the insistence of Jesus was further bloodshed in the form of a general melee avoided.

The unusual facts surrounding the violent scene at Jesus' arrest raise two intriguing questions about the meaning of this story and its relevance to understanding Christ as a criminal defendant. First, what is to be made of Jesus' followers' violence against the arresting party, given their general history of pacifism? Second, what is to be made of the fact that the victim of that violence was a slave, who by definition was disempowered? Both questions reverberate in modern times because violence was not in keeping with Jesus' teachings[1] and because the modern system, like that in place in

Jesus' time, still insulates those who make decisions about criminal law (the chief priest, modern prosecutors) from the risks involved with its enforcement.

In this very small part of the story of Christ the disciples wielded power, and the authorities were the victims of violence. In fact, if Jesus and his followers had been facing a capital sentencing for treason in federal court in the United States, the disciple's actions could have been the basis for the finding of an "aggravating factor," making a death sentence more likely if a jury (quite reasonably) found that attacking a man's head with a sword constituted a "grave risk of danger" to someone who was not killed.[2]

On the very face of the story, it was strange that the disciple, who is identified as Peter in the Gospel of John (18:10), had a sword at all. There were no other instances where the apostles seemed to be armed in public (save at the Last Supper, as discussed below), and their bracingly intentional poverty, which sometimes eschewed even a second tunic to wear while traveling or a bag to hold their possessions, would seem to preclude the possession of military weapons (Matt 10:5-11). More surprisingly, it would appear that the disciple procured the sword at the direction of Jesus, despite his general advocacy of nonviolence. At the Last Supper, Jesus gave the disciples instructions that reversed his previous instructions:

> He said to them, "When I sent you out without a purse, bag, or sandals, did you lack for anything?" They said, "No, not a thing." He said to them, "But now, the one who has a purse must take it, and likewise a bag. And the one who has no sword must sell his cloak and buy one. For I tell you this scripture must be fulfilled in me, 'And he was counted among the lawless'; and indeed what is written about me is being fulfilled." They said, "Lord, look, here are two swords." He replied, "It is enough." (Luke 22:35-38)

Jesus arming his followers? It seems an odd command and inconsistent with his other teachings, including his later condemnation of Peter's use of that same sword to wound the slave (Luke 22:51). Raymond Brown suggests one way to reconcile this apparent conflict. He argues that Jesus was alluding to the change in the lives of the apostles that would come with his death. Up to that point, they had received the direct protection of God, but Jesus knew that after he died, they would experience struggles and persecution unknown to them, and they would need to be ready for trouble.[3] To Brown, the articles Jesus mentioned were merely symbols used to explain the coming change in their lives, and the apostles failed to understand him; Jesus was speaking by symbol and analogy, and as often happened, the apostles took him literally. As Brown puts it, "The items mentioned as preparation, namely, purse, bag, and sword, are quasi-symbolic ways of concretizing the necessary readiness for such contingencies. . . . [T]hat they have in their possession two swords shows they have (mis)understood literally."[4] Brown then goes on to break down the original text of Jesus' response to the production of the two swords ("it is enough") as being an "ironic rendition, equivalent to 'That's the way you normally misunderstand.'. . . One must be wary not to translate the phrase as if Jesus were saying that two swords were enough for the task."[5]

The way Brown understands the scene, it was almost a slapstick comedy—Jesus developed a deep, meaningful, and sober analogy regarding preparedness that mentioned swords, and the apostles at that moment whipped out two swords they somehow procured, as Jesus buried his head in his hands. Could the apostles have so thoroughly misunderstood what Jesus meant? Such a strained reading is almost necessary given Jesus' reaction to the use of the sword at his arrest, however. According to Matthew, it was after cutting off the slave's ear with the sword that the apostle received the famous rebuke from Jesus: "Put your sword back into its place; for all who take the sword will perish by the sword" (Matt 26:52).

Brown's explanation, though, has some problems. For one, this view provides a pretty dim take on the intelligence of Jesus' followers, in that even after Jesus tried to make his meaning clear, they continued to carry literal rather than figurative swords. It would seem that even after months of hearing Jesus preach, they still somehow did not understand his use of parable and symbolism. Of course, as Robert Darden has pointed out, the apostles were quite often boneheaded in their attempts to understand what Christ was telling them through parable and analogy.[6]

Second, and perhaps relatedly, Jesus decried the use of the sword because he knew that his arrest was necessary to fulfill Scripture as the Messiah; at the time of the rebuke (according to John) he asked, "Am I not to drink the cup that the Father has given me?" (John 18:11).[7] He was stopping Peter and the others because he did not want to escape arrest.

There is a third possibility, which may operate together with and not in exclusion of the other theories. It could be that Jesus was not only disappointed to see the sword used, but also particularly distressed to see it used against one of the least powerful persons in the room, a slave. This reading is supported by Jesus' immediate reaction—healing the slave—and by his frequent teachings about poor and powerless persons.

Though some might argue that the slave of the chief priest might have a better life than some others of the time, he was relatively deprived of freedom. Roman law did not generally view slaves as persons, and under the law they had few, if any, rights.[8]

The healing of the slave was unlike many of the other healings performed by Christ in the Gospel of Luke because it was not followed by an acclamation of the act.[9] Instead, this healing was described within the seamless flow of events without special interpretation or comment, almost in passing. Of course, no such acclamation may be needed for such an obvious miracle, or perhaps could not be heard in the ruckus of an arrest. At the least, it was not a grand gesture or one of bravado in the face of power, but instead it was accomplished with a touch of Jesus' hand.

The healing of the slave's ear was unique in perhaps another way: it was the first opportunity for Christ to openly show love for his oppressors, to literally follow his teaching to "love your enemies" (Luke 6:27) once the commencement of truly adversarial actions had begun. He was not healing a follower, the friend of a follower, or someone who begged for his touch; rather, he was healing a member of a crowd that had come to carry his body away so that he might be killed.

It is fair to attach significance to the fact that the injured person who was healed was a slave. Throughout the Gospel of Luke, the dispossessed benefited from Jesus' healing powers, including an unclean man with leprosy (5:12-14), a Roman centurion's servant (7:10), children (8:49-56; 9:37-43), and a disabled woman (13:10-13). His healing of a slave was completely in keeping with his prior choices, which almost exclusively focused on those without status: people with leprosy, servants, children, and women.

Jesus' parables and lessons were consistent with the message conveyed by the persons he chose to heal. Again and again in his teaching, Jesus emphasized the morality and virtue of poor and enslaved people relative to rich and powerful ones. In Luke alone, aside from his frequent denunciations of the powerful religious authorities, he pledged his missionaries to abject poverty (10:1-8), chided the rich in the parable of the Rich Fool who built his wealth only to die (12:13-21), warned against the trappings of power in the wedding parable (14:7-14), and favorably contrasted the poor leper Lazarus with the rich man, as their fates were reversed in heaven (16:19-31).

Perhaps most pointedly, Jesus disappointed a rich ruler who asked Christ what he must do to gain eternal life. The rich ruler, of course, embodied both wealth and power, and told Jesus that he kept the commandments from his youth (Luke 18:21). That was not enough. Jesus told him that he must give up both his wealth and his power by selling his possessions and following Christ (Luke 18:22). In short, he must enslave himself to God. In the end, it should be no surprise that Jesus had contempt for the way his accusers used wealth and power, but compassion for the slave who was forced to do their bidding, even when that order was to take Christ toward crucifixion.

The fact that the sword was used by the disciple to injure a slave rather than a soldier or high priest was not just incidental, as shown by the resulting healing. Rather, it added to the universality of the story in that weapons, whether wielded by those making an arrest or being arrested, are most likely to be used against those with the least power and wealth. It was not the chief priest who was injured;

it was the slave. Today, it is not the police chief or the prosecutor who leads a raid and takes a bullet; it is the rookie cop who is making a third of that chief's salary. As a federal prosecutor, I was discouraged from being present at raids and searches, and few prosecutors tried to directly observe them. In part, the reason was that we were not trained in those procedures, but that would not preclude observation from a distance. Perhaps more influential was a sense among some of us that we were too "valuable" to be present when the arrests were made and the evidence was collected.

The general observation made here—that it is the least among us who are most often put in harm's way—is not limited to the area of law enforcement. In times of war, the great majority of those killed are not those who chose to begin the war, or those who chose how to fight the war, or usually even those who decided to place that unit or those persons in the places where they were killed. The people who are killed are mostly the privates and others who are the followers, not the leaders. This broad disjuncture between those who decide a risk will be taken (the decision makers) and those who die or are injured because the risk was taken (the slaves, privates, and poor persons) sweeps across all levels of society and the horizontal movement of time.

And the least advantaged among us are placed into the hands of executioners today. While the workers making the arrest are disadvantaged relative to others in the law enforcement system perhaps, the death penalty is largely administered to poor, black, feeble, and powerless people.

This fact has been recognized, but not changed, by the Supreme Court of the United States. The crucible moment for the death penalty to date was the Supreme Court's ruling in 1972 that the death penalty statutes of Georgia and Texas were unconstitutional. That case, *Furman v. Georgia*,[10] led to a roughly four-year moratorium on the death penalty until states revised their laws to accommodate the decision. The nine separate opinions of the Supreme Court in *Furman* stand out as particularly impassioned writings. The five opinions holding that the death penalty as applied in Texas and Georgia was unconstitutional focused on the fact that the death penalty is overwhelmingly imposed on poor and relatively powerless people.

Justice William Douglas, for example, based his opposition to the death penalty on the fact that it fell overwhelmingly on the poor and the black members of those eligible for such punishment. In critiquing this disparity, Douglas created a harsh analogy:

> In ancient Hindu law a Brahman was exempt from capital punishment, and under that law, "[g]enerally, in the law books, punishment increased in severity as social status diminished." We have, I fear, taken in practice the same position, partially as a result of making the death penalty discretionary and partially as a result of the ability of the rich to purchase the services of the most respected and most resourceful legal talent in the Nation.[11]

In concurring with Justice Douglas, Justice Thurgood Marshall included statistical tables showing this disproportionate use of capital punishment, and concluded that it is the "poor, the illiterate, the underprivileged, the member of the minority group—the man who, because he is without means, and defended by a court-appointed attorney—who becomes society's sacrificial lamb."[12] Justice Marshall also noted that the problems of poor and black persons in facing capital punishment disproportionately were compounded by political powerlessness, asserting, "So long as the capital sanction is used only against the forlorn, easily forgotten members of society, legislators are content to maintain the status quo, because change would draw attention to the problem and concern might develop."[13]

Sadly, the disproportionate use of the death penalty against poor black persons was not affected by the changes made by states in their capital punishment statutes leading to reinstatement of the death penalty in 1976.[14] In 1987, the Supreme Court revisited the issue in *McClesky v. Kemp*,[15] in which a black defendant claimed racial bias in the Georgia capital system. To support his case, McClesky brought mountains of data showing that black defendants were substantially more likely to be sentenced to death than white defendants charged with the same crime in Georgia, and that the disparity was even greater when black defendants with white victims were compared to white defendants with black victims.

A 5–4 majority held that McClesky's numbers were valid, but that they were not enough to show discrimination in his particular case. In admitting the failure of the courts to remedy the disparities that had been the basis of the ruling in *Furman*, however, the Court recognized the intractability of the states' collective failures to divorce race and class from the machinery of capital punishment.

Part of the problem is not only that juries may be discriminatory, but also that the laws themselves give harsher punishment for the *way* in which poor persons are likely to kill. Specifically, the rich have the ability to commit crimes of greed by financial manipulation, while the poor are more likely to commit such crimes by direct force.

Imagine two killers, for example. One is a poor black man who is robbing a gas station. He has done this successfully before, and he has a loaded gun. In the course of the robbery, the cashier resists, and the defendant shoots him. That robber has now become, at least in some states, eligible for the death penalty, and there is a disproportionate chance that he would receive the death penalty.

His armed robbery is the type of crime that poor people commit because they do not have the means to commit more sophisticated crimes, which might not bring them into contact with other people and the potential for violence on either side. This same criminal, for instance, could get far more money if he were to commit fraud on the Internet by selling fake life insurance. He just does not have the means and training to do so. What he is able to do is to carry a gun into a gas station.

Now consider a rich white man who kills people in a way more typical of his class. He owns a chain of dry-cleaning businesses, and one of the chief costs of doing business is the disposal of toxic chemicals. Imagine now that, like the poor criminal, he wants more money than he has, and he is willing to engage in life-threatening criminal behavior to get it. Instead of going into a business with a gun, the businessman has the option of having the dangerous chemicals dumped into a nearby ditch to save the costs of safe disposal, knowing the chemicals may kill people with wells nearby.

The difference between these two people and their crimes is not the outcome. When the poor man walks into the gas station with a gun and the rich man dumps chemicals into a water supply, both know there is the risk they will end up killing someone. Rather, what distinguishes them is the punishment they are likely to face for that act. The poor black man, as the Supreme Court well knows, is more likely than others to have the death penalty inflicted upon him. And what of the rich white man? If sentenced in federal court and the sentencing guidelines are followed, he will probably receive less than five years in prison.[16] It seems odd that the killer gets less time than the drug buyer, but there is the fact that crack is a drug predominantly used by poor blacks, not rich whites.[17]

There is something, in the midst of all this tragedy and unfairness and violence, that is hauntingly elegant about Jesus' healing touch offered to the slave. Perhaps it is the physical embodiment of what he preached that makes it so powerful. At the least, it reflects his care for those who are disempowered by their society, a care that was made real even in the midst of his own fast and tragic criminal law drama that would end in his death on the cross.

CHAPTER SIX

THE INITIAL APPEARANCE

So the soldiers, their officer, and the Jewish police arrested Jesus and bound him. First they took him to Annas, who was the father-in-law of Caiaphas, the high priest that year.
                                                                    —John 18:12-13

As a criminal law teacher reading the Gospels, I am struck by the sheer amount of *process* that Jesus was afforded. Hurried process, yes, and thoroughly infected by a desire for political outcomes, but process nonetheless. Prior to this deeper study, I thought of the trial and crucifixion as just a mob action, but there is more going on than that. What strikes me, too, is that the process described in the Bible so closely tracks the path of our modern capital defendants. In turn, these bits of process again and again raise the questions we still struggle with today in our courtrooms, law schools, and legislatures.

One almost bizarre example of this synchronicity relates to Jesus' appearance before Annas. The Gospel of John did little to explain why the soldiers took him straight to Annas, other than noting that Annas was Caiaphas's father-in-law. Once there, Jesus basically was asked to explain himself—to plead guilty or not guilty. Jesus refused to do either and was held for further proceedings. The odd thing (to a criminal lawyer) about this seemingly meaningless divergence from the rush to judgment is that it neatly foreshadows an important part of our modern constitutional process, the initial appearance before a magistrate. Further, it presents an eerie prediction of the problems with that modern proceeding—in the role it plays as a premature demand for a plea of guilt or innocence and as a deciding point for continued detention.

Within American law, the initial appearance is not a recent contrivance. Rather, it is a centuries-old product of the Bill of Rights. While the founders seem to have viewed the area of criminal law as being very important, the Constitution as signed in 1787 contained almost no guidance about criminal procedure. Beyond the admonition that all crimes be tried by a jury, it said nothing about how accused criminals should be handled. It was only with the passage of the Bill of Rights in 1791 that criminal procedure was guided by the Constitution. Among those ten amendments, the Sixth Amendment requires that "in all criminal prosecutions, the accused shall enjoy the right . . . to be informed of the nature and cause of the accusation."

In our modern system of criminal law, that passage directs that every person who is arrested is to be brought before a magistrate or other judge as soon as possible, so that the judge may inform her of the charge against her. And to this day in courtrooms across the country, defendants are paraded before magistrates who assure that those defendants are aware of their charges, even if the nature of the charge would be quite evident (for example, the defendant was apprehended fleeing a bank with a mask on his face, a bag of money in one hand, and a gun in the other).

The appearance of Jesus before Annas looks to me, as a lawyer, very much like an initial appearance. At the very least, there are undeniable similarities in both form and function. First of all, like a defendant taken to an initial appearance today, Jesus was taken immediately after his arrest to someone performing the function of a magistrate. Just as Federal Rule of Criminal Procedure 5 requires that "a person making an arrest within the United States must take the defendant without unnecessary delay before a magistrate judge," John reported that Jesus was taken directly to Annas by the soldiers and police. They seemed to know to take him to Annas, even though he was not the chief priest at the time. The Gospel of

John offered no explanation for this detour. Alan Watson specu-
lates that it may have been on Pilate's directions that Jesus was
taken to Annas first, since "Pilate was reluctant to be involved in
any matter that could lead to rioting."[1]

The fact that it was the police and the soldiers (not the Pharisees,
Jesus' many other accusers, or some intermediaries) who delivered
him to Annas, and that those who conducted the trial did not
appear in this portion of the story, is also intriguing and part of the
parallels to modern procedure. Very often, the initial appearance
does not involve advocates for either side; in many jurisdictions it is
rare for either a prosecutor or a defense attorney to show up. Rather,
the initial appearance most often involves only the magistrate, the
defendant, and perhaps the arresting officers (or their reports in
the form of a complaint or arrest warrant affidavit), just as Jesus
appeared alone before Annas, accompanied only by those who
arrested him, and without counsel.

Magistrates who conduct initial appearances in the United
States can take many forms. In Texas, for example, the person serving as a magistrate at an initial appearance can be anything from
a justice of the state supreme court to a justice of the peace or
small-town mayor.[2] The magistrate in this case was Annas, quite an
interesting character. According to John, Annas not only was the
father-in-law of Caiaphas, the high priest, but also was a former
high priest.[3] Annas was the founder of a religious dynasty; five of
his sons, his son-in-law, and a grandson also became high priests.
To gain this position, he had to find the favor of the civil authorities because the high priest of the Jews held his post at the discretion of the Roman governor, who both nominated and deposed the
public religious figures.[4] Annas's role as a prominent judge is found
elsewhere in the New Testament as well. In Acts 4:6, Annas was
one of four judges (including Caiaphas) who served at the trial of
the disciples Peter and John.

The role played by Annas, then, could be seen as similar to the
role of a powerful retired judge serving as magistrate. By my reading of the story, Annas was the first of four judges who dealt with
Jesus. Annas saw him first and took his plea in the manner of a

magistrate; next he was sent to Caiaphas, who served as judge (and prosecutor) at the trial; then to Pilate, as appellate judge; and finally to Herod, as a judge considering a habeas petition.[5]

Today, the magistrate's role includes being called upon to deal with initial appearances by assessing the charges before a defendant, taking a plea from that defendant, and deciding whether to detain or release the defendant pending trial. It was not so different (at least in Jesus' case) two thousand years ago. Imagine the scene. The police and soldiers arrived at a retired official's house with a controversial and well-known figure who was bound in chains. It was the middle of the night, and Annas was roused from bed by the loud knocks on the door. John tells us (after a detour to describe Peter's prevarications) what happened:

> Then the high priest questioned Jesus about his disciples and about his teaching. Jesus answered, "I have spoken openly to the world; I have always taught in synagogues and in the temple, where all the Jews come together. I have said nothing in secret. Why do you ask me? Ask those who heard what I said to them; they know what I said." When he had said this, one of the police standing nearby struck Jesus on the face, saying, "Is that how you answer the high priest?" Jesus answered, "If I have spoken wrongly, testify to the wrong. But if I have spoken rightly, why do you strike me?" Then Annas sent him bound to Caiaphas the high priest. (John 18:19-24)

Certainly, one part of the proceeding diverged from modern practice. Instead of reading the charge to the defendant, Annas tried to question Jesus. What is intriguing, however, is how consistent the story is with a primary aspect of the modern initial appearance—the taking of a plea, in which the defendant may be pressed to declare himself either guilty or not guilty.

The initial appearance in today's real-life courtrooms is not nearly as dramatic as it is sometimes portrayed on television. The reading of the charges is most often given in summary form, with a brief description of the alleged crime. The entry of a plea is similarly perfunctory. It is almost unimaginable that a defendant would plead guilty, at the outset of the case, in the absence of a plea agreement. More than once I have seen defendants, when asked to enter their plea at an initial appearance, announce loudly that they are "guilty!" only to be gently scolded by the magistrate judge and given a second opportunity to plead not guilty.

In many courts, magistrates dodge the initial plea issue by entering a plea of not guilty without asking the defendant for a response. In other courtrooms, defendants are given the option of saying nothing (referred to as standing mute), and a not guilty plea is entered based on the defendant's silence. Thus, to the simple question of "How do you plead?" there are often three possible answers. The defendant may say, "Guilty," "Not guilty," or nothing at all and leave the government to its proofs.

These principles of pleading at the initial appearance can be complex and are still debated. Robert Cochran of Pepperdine Law School, one of the nation's leading experts on law, ethics, and Christianity, has written extensively about the role of the initial plea in the criminal process. In short, Cochran has identified and critiqued the "cruel trilemma" that faces the guilty defendant at his or her initial plea—to lie, to admit guilt, or to remain silent, implying guilt.[6] His view is that pleas of not guilty entered for defendants who are actually guilty undermine the moral authority of the process as a whole because that process is initiated with what is essentially a lie:

> What is for lawyers and judges a casually used term-of-art is viewed by ordinary people as a serious moral claim by the defendant that he did not commit the crime. In order to have his trial, in order to make the state prove its case, the defendant lies. But, of course, the defendant has every right to make the state prove its case against him. He just has to lie about his guilt in order to get that right. At the plea inquiry, the defendant has more a right to lie than a right to remain silent.[7]

To Cochran, the modern American initial appearance is an amoral process, one that "not only conveys the wrong message about the legal system, it violates a host of constitutional norms."[8] I agree with Cochran's condemnation of a proceeding that encourages lying, especially in a proceeding that is the defendant's first contact with the formal criminal justice system. Cochran's preferred solution, which seems eminently reasonable and efficient, is to eliminate the requirement that the defendant enter a plea in the first place. The Constitution does not require it, it serves no real function, and elimination of this step would enhance the efficiency of the courts. Stripping away the entry of a plea by the defendant would not eliminate the initial appearance altogether or affect the constitutional mandate, which directs that the defendant be apprised of the charges, not that he or she enter a plea to them.

Cochran identifies the initial plea as a remnant of the British procedure of several centuries ago, a procedure that was part of an inquisitorial system that respected neither the right to silence nor a presumption of innocence. This remnant obviously does not rest comfortably with the rights of modern American defendants. This historical perspective offers another insight as well; this artifact of British procedure carries us closer to the type of inquisitorial trial that Christ endured, and serves as a wormhole into the pressures that Christ faced while he was a defendant. The accused who squirms under this cruel trilemma today finds himself or herself in the same quandary that Jesus encountered before Annas.

As a lawyer looking at the appearance of Jesus before Annas, I find remarkable Christ's stunning ability to evade the trilemma that Cochran describes. As the defendant, Jesus did not choose any of the three problematic options: he did not admit guilt, he did not claim to be innocent, nor did he remain silent.

Rather, Jesus created a fourth option. He insisted that the authorities come up with evidence on their own: "Ask those who heard what I said to them; they know what I said" (John 18:21). He did it without counsel or assistance, his disciples having fled, and he showed a remarkable resolve, given the persistence and authority of the person who was questioning him, a former high priest and founder of a priestly dynasty. In choosing the path of expressly putting the government to its proofs, Christ implicitly addressed the policy problems that Cochran describes by arguing in favor of exactly the constitutional principle that the trilemma troubles—

the defendant has the right to rest on the presumption of innocence and allow the government to come up with its own evidence rather than try to force a confession from the accused.

Finally, we have another similarity between the modern initial appearance and Jesus' hearing before Annas—the decision to detain the defendant rather than release him. While John did not expressly say whether Annas had the ability to release Jesus, his description ("Then Annas sent him bound to Caiaphas the high priest" [John 18:24]) implied that there was some other course of action possible, and the only other possibility would have been to release him.

John's description could also be read to depict a hearing where the continued detention of Christ was presumed. This take on the story also comes closer to modern practice. In the federal criminal justice system, 18 U.S. Code 3164 establishes a presumption of detention in a broad class of cases, including nearly all drug trafficking cases. Where this presumption exists, a defendant will almost always be bundled off to jail until trial, even though nothing more than probable cause has been shown. When passed in 1984, this presumption was highly controversial because it seemed to run contrary both to the presumption of innocence and to the reasonable bail provision of the Eighth Amendment, which directs that "excessive bail shall not be required." The Supreme Court, however, ruled that the presumption passed constitutional muster. Writing for the majority in *United States v. Salerno*, Chief Justice William Rehnquist held that the presumption clause was merely an "administrative" step to control crime and did not comprise punishment.[9] Of course, one would imagine that to the prisoner cooped up in jail despite the presumption of his or her innocence, the price for that administrative measure is quite high.

Regardless of the amount of leeway that Annas had, the process smells like a finding of detention. Just as magistrates in our courtrooms remand defendants to custody pending trial based on a troubling presumption, Jesus was sent to the next step, still bound in chains. It is intriguing to consider the alternative. What if Annas had released Jesus and told him to return when summoned? Perhaps tempers would have cooled, the crowds of the Passover festival would have dispersed, and there would have been a different, less violent outcome.

In one paragraph within the Gospel of John, the story of Jesus brings to the surface the very issues debated by judges, legal scholars, and practitioners today. Not only was Jesus a criminal defendant, but he was a criminal defendant with a transcendent ability to reveal, critique, and resolve issues that American justice still struggles with in the present moment.

LAST MEAL / LAST SUPPER

While they were eating, he took a loaf of bread, and after blessing it he broke it, gave it to them, and said, "Take; this is my body." Then he took a cup, and after giving thanks he gave it to them, and all of them drank from it. He said to them, "This is my blood of the covenant, which is poured out for many. Truly I tell you, I will never again drink of the fruit of the vine until that day when I drink it new in the kingdom of God." —Mark 14:22-25

A few years ago, I started doing research into the death penalty in Texas. As I delved into newspaper articles on Texas executions, I was struck by a strange anomaly. Almost universally, the news reports on these executions contained a description of the defendant's last meal, listing each component with the solemnity of a fine restaurant's menu. At first, this seemed bizarre. To an attorney, what the defendant ate is completely irrelevant to the story at hand and a trivial diversion in a discussion of a legal process. Continuing to read these stories, though, I found myself looking for that description of the last meal, searching for the menu listing amidst the recounting of horrific crimes and tragedy. In time, the last meals came to seem an essential part of the death drama, regardless of their legal significance. For me, it was the sole point where the convict's life contained an element I could relate to. I could not imagine murdering the neighbors, but I could imagine choosing fried chicken as my last meal. It was a window into the humanity of the condemned person.

I was not alone in my interest in last meals. During the period that the Texas Department of Criminal Justice kept a web log of final meals, it was the most popular feature of that department's website and recorded the final requests of inmates such as Richard Williams, whose final meal included two cheeseburgers, two chili cheese dogs, chocolate cake, apple pie, and three Dr. Peppers.[1] After Texas took such information off its website, a private site called Dead Man Eating began reporting the death menus, complete with a logo showing a man hanging by a noose and holding a dripping ice-cream cone in his hand.

Our society's fascination with last meals seems well served by a variety of media. One can, for example, purchase the book . . . *Last Meal* by Jacquelyn Black, which re-creates several last meals in art-quality photographs, next to descriptions and photos of the convict who requested that meal. Page 58 shows William Prince Davis's last meal (chicken, rolls, chili, a six-pack of Coca-Cola) pictured on clean white porcelain plates with a stark black background.

Perhaps even more compelling is *Meals to Die For*, written by Brian D. Price. Price was an inmate assigned to the Walls Unit in Texas's Huntsville prison, home of that state's death row. For ten years, Price was the cook who prepared the last meals for those executed in Texas, a job he got in part because he had worked in a pizza parlor as a teenager. Price was not on death row; he was serving a fifteen-year sentence for sexual assault.[2] Along with descriptions of those executed and photocopies of the notes containing their last meal requests, Price's book contains recipes for dishes such as Old Sparky's Genuine Convict Chili, Death Chamber Chicken Fried Steak, and Obituary Onion Rings.[3]

More intriguingly, Price describes the role the last meal plays in the final events of a condemned person's life. For example, Karla Faye Tucker requested a relatively simple last meal: fruit and a garden salad with ranch dressing. As many will remember, Tucker's execution was quite controversial despite the severity of her crime (killing two people with a pickax), and the media attention was intense amidst pleas for clemency from world figures including Pope John Paul II. Price writes that even with the added attention, the meal was part of the regular process that preceded each execution. The food was carefully arranged on a plate in the kitchen; then a phalanx of guards delivered it to the part of the prison known as the Death House.[4]

Such details, of course, are only available because of our general fascination with last meals. While the Black and Price books were not best sellers, the same can't be said of Snoop Dogg's 2000 rap album *Tha Last Meal*, which perhaps more clearly shows the iconic nature of such imagery. The cover of the hit record shows a cartoon Snoop Dogg in a prison cell; on one side of the cell door is a priest administering the last rites, and on the other side is a guard delivering a tray of food.[5]

Why is so much attention paid to a last meal? Mike Randleman, the founder of www.deadmaneating.com, speculated that part of the fascination may be fueled by the combination of two primal forces. "Food and death," he noted, "are two of the most emotionally charged things in our lives."[6]

Most of the last meals chronicled are simple meals. That should not be surprising because those making the requests are largely unsophisticated men and women. Jacquelyn Black's photo of the meal chosen by murderer Charles William Bass is typical in its stark simplicity: a few slices of cheese between slices of white bread.[7] Similarly, the picture for Patrick F. Rogers depicts the glass of iced tea he requested as his final meal.[8]

This simplicity takes us back to the Last Supper, the celebrated part of which consisted of bread and wine. While I certainly do not equate the murderers housed in Huntsville with the Son of God, I cannot ignore the fact that the Last Supper was the last meal of a man who knew he would be killed by the state the next day. Nor can one ignore the symbolism of that meal—the Eucharist is perhaps the second most powerful symbol of the faith, behind only the mechanism of execution itself, the cross.

Certainly, there are distinctions between Jesus' last meal and those of the prisoners at Huntsville. For one thing, Christ's last meal was consumed before his conviction and sentence, rather than months or years later. He also chose and ate the meal in freedom with those he loved, rather than being allowed the meal by the very authorities who were about to take his life.

Despite these important differences, there are also important commonalities. Christ, like the Huntsville inmates, knew that he was about to be executed—his cross awaited him as certainly as the Death House awaited Karla Faye Tucker—and that it was to be his last meal. He recognized this fact explicitly in telling the apostles, "I will never again drink of the fruit of the vine until that day when I drink it new in the kingdom of God" (Mark 14:25). Even before the meal, Jesus was aware that it was to be his last. In sending his apostles out to find a place to have the Passover meal that was his last supper, Christ directed his apostles to find a certain man in the city. When they found him, they were to tell the man: "The Teacher says, 'My time is near; I will keep the Passover at your house with my disciples'" (Matt 26:18). Like Karla Faye Tucker (and unlike the rest of us), Christ knew the hour and place he was to die.

Neither Christ nor Tucker needed food; both were about to die, making the idea of nutrition superfluous. The food before Christ and Tucker alike was deprived of its normal function (keeping them alive) and served solely as symbols. For Christ's Last Supper, that symbolism was so strong and powerful that we re-create it regularly in our churches—breaking as a community the bread that became his body, sharing the wine that became his blood. For many Christians, this ritual remains at the center of the practice of the Christian faith.

But what of the symbolism of the Huntsville death row inmate's last meal? Unlike Christ's bread and wine, body and blood, Karla Faye Tucker's fruit does not symbolize God's sacrifice. Yet there is a reason that these meals function so strongly as symbols. As I found in reviewing the descriptions of executions, they represent a link to common humanity. In . . . *Last Meal*, Jacquelyn Black's beautiful photos are moving in part because they depict such ordinary things in the middle of such a dark place: James Russell's single red apple,

Jeffrey Barney's bowl of Frosted Flakes in milk, David Stoker's cheeseburgers nestled in a bed of french fries, all arranged on a plate in the Death House.[9]

To the Christian, one of the most moving acts of God was to place his Son on earth. Similarly, one of the troubling questions facing Christians is why that same God would allow a murderer to kill innocents. In the idea of the last meal, these two things meet. Christ broke the bread at the Last Supper in his two hands, just as we do. It is a tiny bit of commonality we share with one much greater than we are.

The mirror image of this is the last meal of the murderer, one who has committed acts we cannot comprehend. With the murderer we have almost nothing in common (we hope), but still he wants chicken for dinner. It is a tiny bit of commonality we share with one who has made mistakes we cannot imagine.

We are somewhere in between the Savior and the killer. We exist in that wide chasm between the murderer and Christ, yet our common experience meets the murderer in the precise place where it meets the life of Christ. There is an elegant symmetry between the Christ who is perfect beyond our comprehension and the murderer who is flawed beyond our comprehension, and their experiences are like ours in only the most basic of ways. As the murderer picks up the bread, so did Christ, and so do we. Though Christ and the murderer come to us from opposite directions, something inside compels us to try to understand both, and in that attempt to understand we are pulled toward those few brief moments when we share something like the feeling of bread in our hands.

Food—that, we understand.

CHAPTER EIGHT

THE FACT OF A TRIAL

When the day came, the assembly of the elders of the people, both chief priests and scribes, gathered together, and they brought him to their council. —Luke 22:66

A s I began thinking of Jesus Christ as a defendant, several people suggested to me that what occurred before the Sanhedrin was something other than a trial. It was too short, they argued, or too intense, too bitter or political or strange or atypical or quick.

None of those lodging such protests, I noted, had ever tried a case.

I have tried cases. While on the outside a criminal trial may look ordered and somber, the practitioner knows it is most certainly intense and bitter and quick. Each trial is distinct and strange in its own way, and many are stunningly short—major felony trials are often completed in a single day.

No matter how prepared the lawyers may be, a criminal trial is jolting and unpredictable. Consider the position of the prosecutor; at the start of the trial she often will not know what the defense will be, whether the defendant will testify, even whether the defense will present any witnesses at all. She must react on her feet as these facts develop, deflecting each blow from the defense attorney as it arises. There can be nothing orderly about it; the enterprise is largely a mad scramble, even for the most careful and experienced practitioners.

When I read the story of Jesus before the council, I see the elements at the core of a trial: a charge is laid out, evidence is presented, arguments are made, and a verdict is returned. Even if we choose not to call this a trial for some reason, it is so much like a trial that I have no qualms in equating what happened two thousand years ago in Jerusalem to the things I see in the courtrooms of our nation.

Others have paid great attention to whether Christ's trial was a proper Jewish or Roman trial, whether the Sanhedrin had the power to condemn Jesus, and where such a hearing might have been held.[1] Although I have watched these debates with interest, I participate in none of them here. For purposes of my analysis, it does not matter whether the trial was proper or improper, Jewish or Roman. What I find compelling is the trial that occurred. I am drawn by the image of the Savior enmeshed in the very gears I turn as a criminal practitioner.

There are at least four core characteristics of a trial as distinguished from other types of hearings: (1) the existence of a specific charge, (2) the introduction of evidence, (3) arguments about the application of the law to the facts presented, and (4) a decision about the guilt of the accused. It is not necessary to have a jury for a trial; in modern America many felony cases are tried by a judge at the election of the parties. Nor is it necessary that lawyers make the arguments; even today, having rejected their appointed counsel, many felony defendants represent themselves.

Let us examine each of the four characteristics of a trial in turn:

1. The Charge

Jesus stood accused of two separate and distinct crimes. The first was the crime of blasphemy, or the defamation of the name of God, and the second was the threat to destroy the temple in Jerusalem.

According to Leviticus, "one who blasphemes the name of the LORD shall be put to death" (24:16). Thus, this charge would have been a capital offense under the Jewish, if not the Roman, law. From the dialogue described in Matthew 26:63 ("The high priest said to him, 'I put you under oath before the living God, tell us if you are the Messiah, the Son of God'") it seems that the specific blasphemy of which Jesus was accused was a claim that he was the Messiah. The idea that it was a charge is also supported by the fact that the cross was inscribed "The King of the Jews" (Mark 15:26). Theologian Raymond Brown suggests that this label given by the Romans "would have been harmonious with Jesus being called Messiah in his lifetime."[2]

The second charge, which presumably would have been a violation of both Jewish and Roman law, was that Jesus threatened to destroy the temple at Jerusalem. According to Mark, witnesses at the trial claimed, "We heard him say, 'I will destroy this temple that is made with hands, and in three days I will build another, not made with hands'"(14:58). To the Romans, that would have been the more alarming charge of the two, given the violence it implied.

However, the assumption that it was a threat of violence would have ignored Jesus' habit of speaking in parables. Raymond Brown notes that the word (*naos*) used in the Gospels and translated as "temple" actually refers to the sanctuary, the most sacred part of the temple complex.[3] In a sense, the sanctuary was destroyed with Jesus' death as the veil that protected the holy relics was "torn in two, from top to bottom" (Matt 27:51). Without the veil, the sanctuary would no longer serve its central purpose of protecting the relics and the presence of God from the rest of the world. As Brown puts it, "The general function of such a veil would be to shut the holy place off from the profane, and rending the veil would mean destroying the special character or holiness that made the place a sanctuary."[4]

Jesus' being charged with plotting to destroy the temple may well have been a misunderstanding of prophecy—he was plotting not to destroy a building, but to alter its very character and replace its meaning with his three-day journey from death to resurrection.

The fact that it was possibly based on a misunderstanding does not make the trial of Jesus anything less than a trial. Rather, Jesus received a trial on a flawed charge, a creature that is still among us.[5]

2. The Introduction of Evidence

Although the next chapter will address the testimony against Jesus in some depth, it is at least clear that several witnesses testified at the trial. Matthew, for example, described "many" witnesses who testified falsely, followed by two who made specific allegations about the supposed plan for the destruction of the temple (Matt 26:60-61).

Not only was evidence introduced, but it appears to have been introduced pursuant to law. For example, the two witnesses noted by Matthew were not a literary touch (in contrast to Mark's reference to "some" witnesses [Mark 14:57]), but a fulfillment of the requirement in Deuteronomy 17:6 that "on the evidence of two or three witnesses the death sentence shall be executed; a person must not be put to death on the evidence of only one witness."[6] The procedural bar against relying on a single witness is not an ancient relic. Under Texas law, for example, "a conviction cannot be had upon the testimony of an accomplice unless corroborated by other evidence."[7]

As today, the evidence against Jesus (however faulty) was publicly presented in an open forum and in the presence of the accused, and was subject to some threshold of reliability through the requirement of multiple witnesses.

3. Arguments about the Application of the Law

According to the Gospels, both Jesus and his prosecutor, Caiaphas, were able to argue about the application of the law.

Both Mark and Matthew reported Jesus arguing first, followed by Caiaphas. For his part, Jesus seemed to argue that any claim of blasphemy would be proved wrong, given his divinity. When challenged by the high priest, he told the Sanhedrin that he was not guilty—and not guilty because any such claims were true: "'You will see the Son of Man seated at the right hand of the Power,' and 'coming with the clouds of heaven'" (Mark 14:62).

Caiaphas responded with equal passion. "He has blasphemed!" he thundered, referring to Jesus' argument. "Why do we still need witnesses? You have now heard his blasphemy" (Matt 26:65).

As with the modern trial, these arguments were made publicly, after the admission of evidence, and were interactive—the prosecutor, as now, had the last word and used it to turn the defense argument to his advantage.

4. Verdict

After the prosecutor, Caiaphas, gave his closing argument, the jury reached a verdict: "All of them condemned him as deserving death" (Mark 14:64). The use of the word *condemned* (at least in this translation) resounds with criminal practitioners, as it captures the essence of the moment that a verdict is returned. Of the entire trial, that is the most dramatic moment; television dramas that fail to show jury selection or the presentation of evidence always show the moment the verdict is returned. The drama in part draws from the fact that the verdict is the moment in which society, through the jury, condemns the actions of an individual.

Though some might read the trial as a proceeding in which Caiaphas was asking for affirmation of his conclusion, the Gospels don't support this. Caiaphas, concluding his closing argument, ended with the question: "What is your verdict?" (Matt 26:66). That is, he had to ask them for the conclusion; ultimately, they were the ones to condemn the defendant.

The verdict is the purpose of a trial, and in this sad fruition of the process, we see Jesus' ordeal for what it was—a trial.

THE TRIAL WITNESSES

Now the chief priests and the whole council were looking for testimony against Jesus to put him to death; but they found none. For many gave false testimony against him, and their testimony did not agree. Some stood up and gave false testimony against him, saying, "We heard him say, 'I will destroy this temple that is made with hands, and in three days I will build another, not made with hands.'" But even on this point their testimony did not agree.
—Mark 14:55-59

One day in 1996, I went to Detroit's Wayne County jail to meet with a defendant whom I will call John Q. Through his lawyer, Mr. Q. had contacted me requesting a proffer session, in which a defendant offers the government information about his codefendants, hoping that the government will then make him a deal for a lesser sentence in exchange for his testimony. The proffer session is a mating dance of sorts; the prosecutor is looking for evidence, and the potential witness is looking for freedom. The prosecutor (we would hope) wants truthful evidence that will stand up in court, and the defendant wants the largest sentence reduction possible.

The Wayne County jail, built in 1929, has been little improved since that time. The defendant's counsel, the federal agent, and I waited on broken plastic chairs before being shown through several crumbling corridors to an attorney visiting area. When we got there, John Q., wearing his jail-issued jumpsuit and sneakers, looked nervous and anxious to talk to us.

We sat down across the table and exchanged a few pleasantries. I introduced the FBI agent, and we talked a little about the weather outside. After a few minutes, I began to explain my expectations for the proffer session, telling the prisoner that we expected the truth and could not make any promises until we knew what he had to offer. I had barely begun this speech when John Q. cut me off with approximately these words:

JOHN Q.: Enough about all that. What do you want to hear?

ME: I want to hear the truth about what happened, who was involved . . .

JOHN Q.: Well, who do you want to have been involved?

ME: I . . . I just want you to tell me from your own memory who was there.

JOHN Q.: Who do you need to have been there?

ME: Don't make something up. I just want you to tell me the truth.

JOHN Q.: Which truth is it you want to hear?

We didn't use John Q. as a witness. He was too eager to get his sentencing break, and I worried that his multiple truths might turn out to include some that were created on the spot to please my ear. His eagerness to please was part of a pattern that is increasingly apparent and increasingly dangerous to the idea of justice. This is especially true in federal court, where many of the most important criminal conspiracies are prosecuted. As guidelines and mandatory minimums have become harsher, the sentencing break allowed through cooperation has become even more coveted as the only available escape valve in an increasingly merciless sentencing system. Sentencing expert and former prosecutor Frank Bowman remembered one cooperating defendant putting this in graphic terms: "Before, nobody wanted a snitch jacket. Now, everybody rats, man."[1]

In chapter 3, I described Judas as a confidential informant, that is, someone on the street within or with access to a criminal network who provides information to law enforcement in exchange for cash. A confidential informant is different from a cooperating defendant, who is usually under charge and offers testimony in exchange for a lower sentence. John Q., who desperately wanted to become a cooperating defendant, was thus willing to talk in exchange for something more valuable than the money received by Judas and more modern confidential informants: his own freedom. As one might expect, it is a powerful incentive.

One of my favorite legal writers, Ellen Yaroshefsky at Yeshiva University's Cardozo School of Law, has wonderfully described the problems with overeager cooperating defendants through a series of interviews with former assistant United States attorneys in New York. In these interviews, the former prosecutors again and again reveal how cooperators, with or without the aid of the prosecutor, bend facts in order to receive credit for providing useful testimony. She quotes one prosecutor who reveals one way that "truth" can sometimes develop in the course of a discussion between the prosecutor and the cooperating defendant:

> You are now asking a cooperator whether Little Johnny was present at the murder of Big Tony. He thinks and then says yes. He does not seem sure and you give him the spiel about how you only want the truth. By the time he's finished, he has told the detective and the grand jury that Little Johnny was definitely there. Little Johnny is indicted and there is no information except other cooperators to corroborate his involvement.[2]

Another former prosecutor seems to be thinking of cooperating defendants like John Q. when he says:

> Their version of reality is inaccurate. You have to try to understand their predicament and what they think you mean by wanting them to cooperate. Telling them that you just want the truth is meaningless. What is the truth? Truth is very different when

you have lived your life as part of an organization that commits crimes and lived life through deceit. Truth equals what I know or what I can be caught at. Truth depends on how you characterize events in your life.[3]

The cost of using overeager cooperators who lie is nothing short of the worst sort of injustice: the conviction of innocent men and women. In the United States, those who have been wrongly convicted by cooperator testimony include many who were on death row. In the worst instances, prosecutors allowed cases to stand almost solely on the testimony of such cooperators, despite evidence that the defendants were innocent. For example, Ron Williamson came within five days of execution after being convicted of rape and murder with the primary evidence against him being the testimony of a jailhouse cooperator. To preserve the effect of this testimony, the prosecutors in that case hid (among other exculpatory evidence) the confession given by another man.[4]

Intriguingly, the problem of unreliable, overeager witnesses combined with some sloppy legislative drafting led to a shocking, but brief, period in which it appeared that almost all federal prosecutors might be committing felonies simply by soliciting the testimony of cooperating defendants. In 1998, the United States Circuit Court for the Tenth Circuit, based in Denver, held that giving sentencing breaks to cooperators was in violation of federal law. In that case, *United States v. Singleton*,[5] the court of appeals read a federal statute, 18 U.S. Code §201(c)(2-3), to mean what it said:

> Whoever . . . directly or indirectly, gives, offers, or promises anything of value to any person, for or because of the testimony under oath or affirmation given or to be given by such person as a witness upon a trial, hearing, or other proceeding, before any court . . . authorized by the laws of the United States to hear evidence or take testimony . . . shall be fined under this title or imprisoned for not more than two years, or both.

In short, the Tenth Circuit panel held that it was a felony for prosecutors to offer cooperating defendants a break on their sentence in exchange for their testimony.

The period in which *Singleton* held sway lasted only a few months, until the Tenth Circuit met as a whole and heard from panicked government attorneys claiming that the system of justice would erode without cooperating defendants. That court then reversed course and decided that such breaks, in fact, did not violate the plain meaning of the law.[6] The constant figure of the eager cooperator survived and remains a fixture in American criminal justice.

It may seem a stretch to bridge the problems presented by cooperators in American criminal law to the trial story in the Gospels. Nowhere in the Bible does it clearly say that those testifying against Christ were doing so for the benefit of money or personal freedom.

However, if we look at the story as a whole, it may not be such a stretch. In the end the witnesses against Christ may well have been more like the cooperating defendants of today than they first appear. Matthew made it clear that the prosecutors of Jesus were not just seeking witnesses, but those who would be willing to lie in order to get a conviction: "Now the chief priests and the whole council were looking for false testimony against Jesus so that they might put him to death" (Matt 26:59). Thus, the prosecutors weren't looking for the truth; rather, they were looking for those willing to tell the "truth" they wanted to hear, the kind of witness that one might find in the Wayne County jail.

To understand the witnesses recruited by Caiaphas, we need to start with the revelation that the prosecutors of Christ were specifically looking for *false* testimony. It seems unlikely that volunteers would step forward to lie in court for no apparent reason. Only pathological people tell lies recreationally or as a matter of course. In reality, most people lie to receive some benefit or to avoid some harm. Given the apparently large numbers of people that Caiaphas found to testify falsely against Jesus, it would seem that he must have been offering such a benefit or threatening harm if they did not testify as he wanted. The benefit might have been money, like that received by confidential informants today. Similarly, the threatened harm might have been imprisonment, the same threat that cooperating defendants are attempting to dodge as they take the stand in our courtrooms every day. And just as with modern cooperators, their very eagerness marked them as problematic.

As Matthew described it, "many false witnesses came forward" (26:60). The imagery this conjures up is compelling—a surge of witnesses willing to lie about or misconstrue what Jesus had said. Again, there is an echo of the way in which Ellen Yaroshefsky has described the modern cooperation process: "There is often what is commonly referred to as a 'race to the station house' to obtain a cooperation agreement."[7]

This race to testify among the witnesses against Jesus, like the eagerness of modern cooperators, did not lead unfailingly to the revelation of truth. Instead, as Mark noted, "their testimony did not agree" (14:56). Although the Bible does not make clear how the witnesses disagreed, it may well have been differences in describing what Jesus said, and when and where he said it. Matthew described the order of questioning somewhat more clearly, suggesting that the parade of false witnesses concluded with the two who directly accused Jesus of threatening to tear down the temple (Matt 26:60-61). Even those two, though, according to Mark 14:59, did not agree on the details of the offense.

If the prosecution had tried, could they have found a decent witness? Mark 14:66-68 described how one such potential witness evaded testifying. Remember as you read this familiar passage that at the time, Jesus was awaiting or undergoing trial, and the high priest was desperately trying to round up witnesses:

> When Peter was below in the courtyard, one of the servant-girls of the high priest came by. When she saw Peter warming himself, she stared at him and said, "You also were with Jesus, the man from Nazareth." But he denied it, saying, "I do not know or understand what you are talking about."

Could it be that the high priest's servant approached Peter as a potential witness at the trial? We do not know that this was definitely the case, but it fits with the context of the scene. This possibility certainly casts Peter in a better light; it could be that he was protecting Jesus by avoiding a situation where he would be forced to testify to what he truly believed—that Jesus was the Son of God.[8]

Is Peter's ability to avoid testifying a reflection of our modern process? Is taking the easy way out and relying on witnesses who are there to earn a reward of some type good enough? To answer these questions, we must answer tough questions about costs and efficiency.

Our modern reliance on cooperators is borne of the same impulse that led Caiaphas to recruit unreliable witnesses: We don't want to spend the time and money necessary to get better evidence, and we worry that requiring more neutral evidence may lead to the acquittals of those we would like to convict, imprison, and sometimes execute.

Is the use of cooperators out of hand? To this question, I offer a single statistic. In 1998, more than 63 percent of the narcotics-trafficking defendants tried in the federal Eastern District of Pennsylvania received a break at sentencing for cooperating with the government.[9] Think about that—*more than half* of the defendants in that type of case were cooperating.[10] Who, then, were they informing on? Apparently, they mostly ended up pointing to the 37 percent of defendants who did not get such a break. A system so reliant on cooperators motivated by personal interest is not efficient; it is broken.

Perhaps, as in Jerusalem two thousand years ago, we need fewer paid-off cooperators and more diligent servant girls in the courtyards looking for those who can and will tell the truth.

CHAPTER TEN

THE PROSECUTOR'S EMOTION

Then the high priest tore his clothes and said, "He has blasphemed!
Why do we still need witnesses? You have now heard his blasphemy.
What is your verdict?" —Matthew 26:65-66

Yelling, demanding a verdict, even tearing at his clothes—
Jesus' prosecutor, as described by Matthew, was frustrated.
And no wonder! First, the trial came after several failed
attempts to trick Jesus into statements that could be considered
blasphemy. Now, having arrested Jesus without such evidence, the
prosecutor searched desperately for witnesses who would say what
he wanted (Matt 26:59). When he finally found a sufficient number, they testified in a way that was too obviously false and conflicting, requiring the production of even more witnesses (Matt
26:60; Mark 14:56). Finally, the prosecutor put Jesus under oath
(Matt 26:63) and compelled his testimony, but Jesus answered the
prosecutor's claim that he had committed blasphemy with a riddle:
"You have said so. But I tell you, / From now on you will see the
Son of Man / seated at the right hand of Power / and coming on the
clouds of heaven" (Matt 26:64). The confusing parade of conflicting witnesses, the riddle spun by the defendant—it should come as
no surprise that the prosecutor turned to emotion to sway the jury
to his side.

Frustrated people tend to overreact. Prosecutors may lash out
against defendants in their arguments despite the fact that their

primary duty is "not to convict, but to see that justice is done."[1] Dramatic shows of prosecutorial rage are well documented in our time. The United States Supreme Court case of *Darden v. Wainright*[2] describes a prosecutor who may well have been on the verge of tearing his clothes. He was prosecuting a capital case and was seeking the death penalty, and he was frustrated with the defense attorney's challenge to his proofs. When his turn came, the prosecutor in that case ranted that he wished, "I could see [the defendant] sitting here with no face, blown away by a shotgun," and "I wish he had been killed in the accident, but he wasn't," among other inflammatory statements.[3] Although this method of prosecution by emotion was condemned by the Florida Supreme Court, the federal district court, the federal court of appeals, and the Supreme Court itself,[4] the holding of the Supreme Court majority was that such stoking of the fires of emotion "did not deprive petitioner of a fair trial."[5]

Caiaphas, of course, relied on more than angry words to signal his anger and to express himself to the jury—he tore his clothes, something we cannot imagine a lawyer doing today. This may seem like an extreme action to us in the modern day, yet it was a more common expression of public anger at that time. For example, Licinius Regulus tore his clothes in the Roman Senate when he heard he was not on the list of selected members, and Augustus, the Roman emperor, tore his apparel when he heard about the defeat of his general, Varus, in Germany.[6] The scene is rendered all the more dramatic by the chance that Caiaphas was wearing ceremonial vestments.

It wasn't just the tearing of clothes that signaled the prosecutor's frustration, though. Consider his use of a rhetorical question as an accusation. "Why do we still need witnesses?" Caiaphas asked the jury, urging the trial to a close. Those six words, in their bare simplicity, exposed the raw emotion of the moment; it is hard to say those words without an edge in the mind's voice, without an urgency and pathos fitting the moment. Caiaphas was urging not only a conclusion but also that the verdict be returned *now*, while that wave of emotion still ran hot. That much is clear from his words.

There is one more, somewhat hidden, clue that Caiaphas rode Jesus to conviction on the embers of emotion. We know that the council, acting as the jury, was unanimous in convicting him: "All of them condemned him as deserving death" (Mark 14:64). It appears that the decision of this jury was immediate, following on the heels of Caiaphas's performance in the well of the court, the strips of cloth perhaps still lying on the floor beneath him.

The clue lies in those jurors, the ones who decided quickly in the heat of the moment. As the scene was described, the events happened in rapid-fire succession: Caiaphas whipped himself into a retributive frenzy, asked for an immediate condemnation, and received it. There might not have been a moment for reflection or discussion; the vote was taken and the deed was done.

One might imagine that in such a situation, one symptom of this unjust process might be conflicted jurors who, once beyond the passion of the moment, had second thoughts or regrets about the decision they made. Exactly this scenario played out in Christ's trial in the person of Joseph of Arimathea, whom Mark identified as "a respected member of the council" (Mark 15:43). Despite having been one of those who condemned Jesus, he appeared to have had second thoughts after the crucifixion. Upon hearing of the completion of Jesus' death, he "went boldly to Pilate and asked for the body of Jesus" (Mark 15:43). Pilate gave him the body, and Joseph bought a linen cloth, wrapped the body, and placed it in a tomb that may well have been the one hewn for his own burial (Mark 15:46). Mary Magdalene watched as the body was placed there (Mark 15:47), and one can only imagine what she thought as she observed a member of the jury who condemned Jesus wrap the body of the condemned man and place it in his own place of honor. Perhaps what she saw was an act of contrition by a juror who had been too easily swayed by the emotions of a prosecutor.

Unfortunately, emotions such as anger and contrition, so much a part of our lives, are too rarely examined when we look at the law. We law professors often teach the law as a dry, staid, and intellectual pursuit. Through the idea of relevance, law students are made to read cases that delve deeply into the reasoning of courts on minute legal distinctions, but often fail to even acknowledge the people and the tragedy that lie behind every case brought to the attention of a court. Professor Susan Bandes (one person who has tried to remedy this deficiency) has asserted that the language of legal theory "is not language that tends to welcome or even acknowledge emotion. On the contrary, it tends to pride itself on its ability to rise above the pull of emotion."[7] She also recognizes why legal theory discounts emotion: "Emotion is variable, messy, interdisciplinary, soft and feminine, fact-based, difficult to categorize, non-rational—in short it has all sorts of attributes that interfere with a claim for overarching, transcendent status."[8]

This turning away from the role of emotion in our legal systems is also a departure from our roots. In part, Aristotle's *On Rhetoric* was written as a response to other handbooks of rhetoric that were created to aid those speaking in the law courts of Greece.[9] Classical rhetoric in those courts was largely and expressly based on the manipulation of emotions, and Aristotle devoted a large part of *On Rhetoric* to a discussion of emotion and how it is aroused.[10] Aristotle's commentary on the use of emotion shows the timelessness of those emotions; for example, he suggested that "a kind of pleasure follows all experience of anger from the hope of getting retaliation. . . . It has been well said of rage, 'A thing much sweeter than honey in the throat, it grows in the breast of men.'"[11] That same flavor of rage and its fruits lingers in the wake of today's capital convictions, sometimes in the voice of the sad survivors who talk about closure and retribution.

Thousands of years after Aristotle wrote those words, the modern legal academy discounts the importance of emotion, but practitioners do not. As a prosecutor, I knew that from the start of a trial to the end, emotion had very much to do with the outcome. In choosing jurors, we would look for those whose experiences would, through the emotion of empathy, pull to our side. In our opening statements, we were taught to tell the story of the case in a whole and real way so that it would engage the emotions of the

jurors from the outset. When I put a victim on the stand as a witness, I would not stop or comfort her if she started to cry because I
knew the effect that her tears were having on the jury. When cross-
examining defense witnesses, I was trying to manipulate their emotions, too, by making them angry and frustrated so that their stories
would break down. Finally the closing would come, and I would try
to create a whole range of emotions: empathy for the victim, anger
at the defendant, admiration for the police officers who investigated the case, and frustration that nothing had been done about
the defendant sooner. While the law professors and courts may
wring the law dry of emotion, those who tell the stories of the case
know better about what is the heart of justice.

One thing about all that management of emotion is that it can
be very hard to turn off. And becoming emotional about the case
leads to something very dangerous for the prosecutor—a loss of perspective about the facts and overcommitment to the outcome of
conviction. At worst, the prosecutor keeps pushing against a defendant even after it should be clear that the defendant probably did
not commit the crime.

This phenomenon was played out by the prosecutors in Jefferson
County, Alabama, who were charged with bringing the case against
Ronnie and Dale Mahan, accused of abduction and rape. They
took the brothers to trial and presented a case that relied on the
testimony of the victim. The jury accepted the prosecutors' arguments and convicted both men.[12]

After the trial of the Mahans, the prosecutors' problems began,
however. DNA testing showed that they could not be the sources
of the semen recovered from the victim after the alleged assault,
and the judge granted a new trial. Undeterred by this fact, the prosecutors prepared for retrial under the theory that the rapist had not
ejaculated, and that the semen was from the victim's husband. This
theory fell apart, too. The semen was subjected to DNA analysis
again and found not to match the DNA of the victim's husband.[13]

Even at that, the prosecutors did not waver. The victim then told
the prosecutors that the semen was not from a rapist or from her
husband, but from a boyfriend with whom she also had sex that day.

This theory dissolved when hair analysis showed that the boyfriend claim wasn't true, either. Finally, the victim (having been caught in a series of lies) stopped cooperating with the prosecutors and refused to testify.[14]

One would think at that point the prosecutors would at least have had some doubts about their conclusions. One would be wrong. After all of these events, after the disproving of each of their theories, and after the dismissal of their case against the Mahans, one prosecutor described his commitment to guilt: "[They] are guilty as sin. There's no question in my mind. This is not a case of innocence. . . . [They] are guilty. I just can't prove it."[15]

Susan Bandes suggests that the overcommitment of prosecutors to conviction can be explained in part by the "context of the actual people with whom the prosecutor works,"[16] including victims, police officers, other prosecutors, and supervisors—all of whom encourage a total and heartfelt commitment to the project of convicting those who are charged. At the same time, ethical rules and the culture of the prosecutor's office keep the prosecutor away from those who might provide a more complete picture—the defendant, his or her family, and his or her witnesses. As Susan Bandes puts it, "The person whom the prosecutor does not get to know intimately is the defendant."[17]

Ellen Yaroshefsky noted the same problem of a peer group that tended to reinforce belief in guilt, even when the facts should undermine that confidence. While studying prosecutors in New York, she was told by one former prosecutor that some in the office were "true believers" who "most identify with law enforcement and could never imagine that they would be defense attorneys. They tend not to see gray in situations. It is all black and white. There's not a healthy difference between their role and that of the agents."[18]

Just as modern prosecutors can be drawn into an irrational emotional commitment to their cases through their peers, the same could well have been true of Caiaphas. As Raymond Brown described him, he was part of a relatively insular "Jerusalem priestly aristocracy with positions of privileged power over the Temple and its treasury."[19] A simple analogy seems to fit. In the same way that Bandes and Yaroshefsky link prosecutors' sometimes irrational connection to their cases to their isolation from those they prosecute, so Caiaphas would have been isolated from outsiders such as Jesus and his followers.

Caiaphas manipulated the emotions of his audience; so does the modern prosecutor. So what? Is there a cost associated with that dynamic? Should the decision of guilt be made on some other basis than that which we employ to decide so many of the other crucial decisions in our lives? After all, many of us have decided whom to marry, what job to take, or what house to buy based on a momentary emotion that seized us at precisely the right time, often having been put in that emotional state by someone who wanted us to make that decision.

So why not jury trials, too? The simple answer is that a verdict based on emotional response is contrary to the core purpose of trial itself, which is to determine truth. In a case in which identity of the perpetrator is at issue, the fact that the crime committed enrages us does not mean that the defendant committed it; yet the prosecutor is likely to conclude her or his summation with exactly those descriptive words that will engage our anger. To do so distracts a jury from the true question at hand no less than Caiaphas's tearing of his clothes distracted the jury from Jesus' innocence; yet we tolerate it. Perhaps as we celebrate the passion of Christ, we should also see the tragic passions of the prosecutor and recognize the shadowy dangers they create.

CHAPTER ELEVEN

THE APPEAL TO PILATE

As soon as it was morning, the chief priests held a consultation with the elders and scribes and the whole council. They bound Jesus, led him away, and handed him over to Pilate. Pilate asked him, "Are you the King of the Jews?" He answered him, "You say so." Then the chief priests accused him of many things. Pilate asked him again, "Have you no answer? See how many charges they bring against you." But Jesus made no further reply, so that Pilate was amazed.
—Mark 15:1-5

Once the council convicted Jesus, something odd happened. We would expect that he would be taken out and the punishment would be exacted—he would be killed without any further process. That certainly would have been in keeping with the speed and fervor of the events to that point. What else would we expect after Caiaphas whipped the crowd into a retributive frenzy? If we think about that scene, it is easy to imagine the crowd following eagerly to see an immediate execution in the courtyard.

But for some reason, that did not happen; instead, Jesus was given a second hearing, that time in front of a single judge. Like the initial appearance before Annas, the appeal to Pilate tracks modern practice and raises the same questions that we see in modern appeals. Specifically, critics of our criminal justice system contend that while appeals can sometimes catch procedural problems, they do a lousy job of ensuring basic fairness, especially when prosecutors overreach. Too often an appeal ensures only that an unfair result was gained through the use of proper procedures. As with the other aspects of the process, what happened to Jesus on appeal is significant not only in being an important event, but also in pointing to some failures in our system of justice. Jesus got a lot of process, but not much justice, a position familiar to those within our country who have been exonerated of crimes through DNA evidence—exonerated after not only a conviction but also an appeal.

The four Gospels of the Bible diverged in their descriptions of the hearings that followed the council's decision, though each sketched some form of postconviction proceedings. All of the Gospels except John described the trial before the council, and all included an appearance before Pilate (Matt 27:11-14; Mark 15:1-5; Luke 23:1-5; John 18:28-38). After that point, the Gospels diverged further. Luke (alone) noted that Pilate heard Jesus' case, then sent him on to Herod while apparently making no decision at that time (Luke 23:6-7). It is this hearing before Herod that I compare to a habeas proceeding in the following chapter. The other three Gospels skipped that event. All four Gospels, however, included Pilate's offering the crowd clemency for either Jesus or the bandit Barabbas (Matt 27:15-23; Mark 15:6-15; Luke 23:13-25; John 18:39-40), which I delineate in chapter 13 as a clemency hearing. To draw a lesson from each of these elements of the story, I have fit them together in order to best understand them in a modern context. I don't claim this is historically proved or a necessary reading, but it certainly is one among many ways to understand these passages. Thus, I assume that Jesus first was tried by the council, then had an appeal before Pilate, a habeas hearing before Herod, was returned to Pilate for a clemency hearing, and finally was executed by Roman authorities.

Though the Gospels told different parts of the story, each described a surprising amount of postconviction activity. This confusing array of postconviction events is in itself something that Jesus' experience had in common with the modern defendant. For many defendants, the conviction at trial is the start, not the end, of the battle. The modern defendant (assuming no subsequent petitions) may have no less than ten separate hearings: the trial, an appeal, a further appeal to that state's supreme court, a petition before the United States Supreme Court, then habeas petition hearings before the trial court, the state court of appeals, the state supreme court, the federal district court, the federal court of appeals, and finally back to the U.S. Supreme Court on the habeas issues.

Perhaps it strikes us as odd that Jesus received an appeal (and later, the equivalent of a petition for habeas corpus) because, like the initial appearance before Annas, it seemed like so much *process* within the midst of what seemed like an anarchic or tyrannical system. As fast and arbitrary as they were, Jesus' trial and posttrial hearings seemed relatively orderly when held up against the other state execution described in the Gospels, that being the beheading of John the Baptist. There, Herod sent his troops out to throw John in prison without trial after John accused Herod of stealing his brother's wife (Mark 6:17-18). He did that on the direction of the stolen wife, but later came to enjoy talking to John and feared him as a righteous and holy man (Mark 6:20). It is a compelling visual image—the king and the captive talking, with the captive challenging the morality of the ruler at every turn. In the end, the king promised his daughter anything she wanted, and she asked for the head of John the Baptist, which Herod promptly delivered to her in the middle of a feast (Mark 6:22-28). Now *that* was a lack of process!

The idea of a case being appealed is a key to our contemporary sense of justice. An appeal serves at least two primary purposes. First, the availability of appeal offers a chance to undo any wrongful or improper decision made by a jury or trial judge. It recognizes the fallibility of the justice system and slows down the process for deliberation before fresh eyes. Second, an appeal allows for standardization in a given justice system, in that the appellate court can insist that lower courts act uniformly in similar situations. The appellate courts keep each trial court from developing a common law of its own.

Anyone who doubts the importance of appeals in the United States needs only to consider the very structure of our courts. In the federal system, and most of the states, the structure is the same. At the bottom of the hierarchy are the trial courts, where facts are determined and decisions made in both civil and criminal cases. At this point civil litigants are awarded damages (or not), and criminal defendants are acquitted or found guilty and then sentenced. It is only at this bottom level that evidence is gathered. Above these trial courts are *two* levels of appellate courts. The loser at the trial level can appeal the case to the first level of appeals, which in the federal system is the court of appeals for the circuit in which the trial court sits.[1] But even that is not the end—the loser in the court of appeals can petition to the United States Supreme Court for further review of the matter.

The importance given to appeals is reflected in the status accorded to the judges at these different levels. The most prestigious and powerful is the Supreme Court. Confirmation to the United States Supreme Court can be a political battle, and those who succeed in making it to the Supreme Court are given high honor and the unique title of justice. They are most often chosen from the ranks of the judges sitting on the courts of appeal, who in turn are often (though not always) drawn from the body of federal trial judges. Thus, it is a promotion to go from trial judge to appellate judge, and the advantages coming with that promotion are significant. Not only do appellate judges have more status and pay, but they avoid the drudgery of long hours watching trial. Rather, they hear relatively short arguments by the parties or their lawyers, then ponder their decisions at their leisure. It is, in short, a position with all the trappings of power—the same sort of power that Pilate seemed to enjoy.

In describing the first appearance of Jesus before Pilate as an appeal, I do not mean to suggest that any of those involved would necessarily have considered it to be an appeal, or that such an appeal was required under Roman law. Rather, I use the word *appeal* to describe this hearing because it fits what we would consider an appeal in the modern context, and I can't imagine what else to call it, given that the jury had already condemned the defendant and sentenced him to death (Matt 26:66), and a person with the authority to reverse the decision was given a chance to review the facts and decision in the case. Whether it was termed an appeal to Romans or Jews of the time isn't known, but I am confident that in holding up this experience to modern process, the American lawyers of today would call it an appeal, nothing more and nothing less. Nearly all the writing on the trial of Christ has (not surprisingly) been done by biblical scholars, and they almost universally refer to the hearing before Pilate as a trial. This does not ring true to me as a lawyer who has tried cases and argued appeals.

Others have suggested that what happened before Pilate was more a confirmation of the council's judgment rather than a new trial, including J. Steller in 1674. Some of these earlier scholars referred to Pilate's actions as a *recognitio causae*, which is "an inquiry to see if the accusation in the previous trial was justified and a determination of the details of the penalty."[2] In considering this question, Raymond Brown takes into account the setting of the hearing. Pilate ruled a new imperial province in a time of transition between the Roman republic and the beginning of the Roman Empire, and that province did not have many Roman citizens seen as deserving full legal rights. Thus, less formal processes probably were employed.[3] Brown seems to accept that what occurred was likely a *cognitio*, which is a hearing somewhere between a simple affirmation and a full trial in terms of formality. As Brown puts it, this would allow Pilate to "draw information from local authority without requiring the kind of proof demanded by the ordinary law."[4] Though Brown then uses the term *trial* to describe the hearing, none of the facts he presents would distinguish this process from an appeal, where the court of appeals is often far off geographically from the local events and relies almost entirely on the facts developed in the case below.

In relation to that evidence, when Raymond Brown and others describe the hearing before Pilate as a "trial,"[5] the reason may be that Pilate considered the evidence presented below by the defendant (and repeated before Pilate) rather than just legal issues. In fact, this is not unusual for an appeal. Commonly, what is challenged on appeal by a criminal defendant is the sufficiency of the evidence in the trial below, and that was precisely what Pilate seemed to weigh as he considered the appeal of Jesus.

Another reason that some argue the proceeding before Pilate should be considered a trial is that, because the crucifixion was to be carried out by Romans, it needed the authorization of that more powerful authority. Some biblical scholars hold that even if the Jewish authorities were capable of sentencing a defendant to death, they did not have the ability to carry out the execution.[6] Thus, an appearance before Pilate was necessary to fulfill the judgment. Again, this does not create a distinction from modern practice if we consider the hearing before Pilate to be an appeal. The Supreme Court has held that a criminal trial has the right to an appeal; thus, a state does not have the ability to order an execution until after the appellate court has affirmed the conviction and sentence. By this reading, the appellate court in the United States plays the role of Pilate, a necessary stop on the road to execution.

But does it *matter* in the end whether we think of what happened before Pilate as an appeal rather than a trial? It does if we seek to apply the words and lessons of the Gospel to our contemporary world. Like a modern appellate court, Pilate was a separate and independent entity from the body that conducted the trial. Like a modern appellate court, Pilate seemed to have superior authority— that is, the ability to reverse the decision of the council below. And finally, like a modern appellate court, Pilate refused to actively question the intentions of the prosecutors and deferred to them over his own conscience.

Procedurally, Pilate even acted like a modern appellate court. He first questioned Jesus directly ("Are you the King of the Jews?" [Mark 15:2]).[7] While many imagine oral argument at the appellate level to be the careful giving of speeches by the parties, it is often more like the questioning that Jesus faced. In my experience, I have more than once been questioned by the judges of a court of appeals before the first word emerged from my mouth. In one notably disastrous appearance before the United States Sixth Circuit Court of

Appeals, the chief judge began yelling questions before I had even entered the well of the court. Usurpation by a powerful judge is neither ancient nor modern; rather, it seems to be eternal.

After hearing from Jesus, Pilate heard the arguments of the prosecution, in the role of the appellees (Mark 15:3). They apparently did not limit themselves to the immediate question and instead accused Jesus of "many things" (Mark 15:3). Once the chief priests had their say, Pilate turned back to Jesus, asking, "Have you no answer?" (Mark 15:4).

What is remarkable about this exchange (at least as described in the Gospel of Mark) is that the dialogue follows the exact progression observed in an American appellate court. In modern appellate practice the loser in the trial below, referred to as the appellant, is allowed to speak first. Here, as the defendant convicted by the council, Jesus would be in the role of appellant, and he was allowed to speak first. Next, by modern practice, the appellee (or opponent of the appeal) is given a chance to make argument, and that was precisely what Pilate allowed. Finally, in our courts and before Pilate, the appellant is allowed to make rebuttal argument. Strikingly, "Have you no answer?" is a wonderful invitation to such rebuttal.

Having heard the arguments, Pilate clearly had the power to release Jesus. However, he did not use that power; rather, he decided not to alter the decision of the court below in favor of the prosecution. Again, his actions tracked those of the American judiciary. The tendency of American appellate courts to side with the government is particularly pronounced. For example, the federal government wins the great majority of the appeals of sentences taken to the court of appeals, both when it seeks to have a sentence affirmed (when the defense says it is too high) and when it seeks to have one reversed as too low. This is true even when the appellate court clearly thinks that something is morally wrong with the prosecution. For example, in one case appealed to the federal Fifth Circuit Court of Appeals, a woman in her fifties received what was effectively a life sentence (forty-five years in prison without a chance of parole) for a first and nonviolent gun-possession and narcotics conviction.[8] This lengthy sentence resulted entirely from the way the prosecution chose to charge the case, by breaking the charges into separate counts. The court recognized that this technique results in "astonishingly long" sentences and gave prosecutors the ability to unfairly pressure defendants into guilty pleas. Nonetheless, the appellate court affirmed the sentence and sent the woman off to die in prison.[9]

If appeals almost always go the way of the prosecution, before Pilate or the federal courts of appeal, what is the big deal about appeals? In part, it might be the very act of affirming the state that lends legitimacy to the system as a whole. It creates the perception, if not always the reality, of a certain, contemplative system that has checked every fact. After all, Jesus was brought before three decision makers (Caiaphas, Pilate, and Herod), and all of them allowed the execution to proceed; thus, he must have been guilty. This logic, of course, requires that we have utter faith in the process of humans reviewing facts, and some within our own system have that utter faith. For example, former Florida governor Jeb Bush justified his opposition to abortion and support for the death penalty through the familiar shibboleth that "taking an innocent life is wrong."[10] This formula works only if you assume, as Governor Bush does, that the criminal justice system is perfect and would not result in the execution of an innocent.

The formality of the appellate court helps build this perception of perfect results. If you ever have the chance to attend an argument before the United States Supreme Court, you will see this at work. The chamber is somber and grand, and there is an expectant hush before the justices enter the room. It is one of the few public spectacles where men in the audience still wear coat and tie, and visitors are seated by marshals in uniform. Those presenting argument before the court are formally dressed, and the entire production comes to resemble Kabuki theater, but for the vigorous debate that sometimes ensues. Only a slightly less formal atmosphere attends the proceedings of the courts of appeal.

While Pilate might not have enjoyed exactly the same trappings of power, he did have the power to change the judgment below, and through inaction, he declined to use that power. But why did he decline to act? Luke reported that Pilate seemed convinced that there was not enough evidence. After hearing from the chief priests, he concluded, "I find no basis for an accusation against this man" (Luke 23:4). Yet he still declined to reverse the conviction, at least in part because of the insistence of the crowd (Luke 23:5).

Why would Pilate maintain the status quo even in that instance? After all, like anyone facing our unelected and life-tenured federal appellate judges, those petitioning him had no power to challenge his position—he held that post at the hand of Rome (or Washington), not of the local population. Nevertheless, he deferred to their insistence.

Appellate courts sometimes sort the bad convictions from the good. However, our faith that they ensure justice may be unfounded. The judges are women and men, after all, subjected to the same social pressures of everyone else, pressures that sometimes lead to the popular and retributive outcome over the right one. Pilate had a room full of accusers before him as he pondered his decision, a striking symbol of the public desire for retribution that may in a less visible way be hovering like a mist in the back rows of appellate courtrooms in our time and place.

CHAPTER TWELVE

HABEAS DENIED

When Pilate heard this, he asked whether the man was a Galilean. And when he learned that he was under Herod's jurisdiction, he sent him off to Herod, who was himself in Jerusalem at that time. When Herod saw Jesus, he was very glad, for he had been wanting to see him for a long time, because he had heard about him and was hoping to see him perform some sign. He questioned him at some length, but Jesus gave him no answer. The chief priests and the scribes stood by, vehemently accusing him. Even Herod with his soldiers treated him with contempt and mocked him; then he put an elegant robe on him, and sent him back to Pilate.

—Luke 23:6-11

Though only the Gospel of Luke described Pilate sending Jesus to Herod, it was a compelling turn of events. Herod represented a different sovereign than Pilate did, had the ability to free Jesus, and elected not to do so despite the apparent innocence of the prisoner. In each of these ways, the story tracks the appearance of a condemned state prisoner appearing in federal court seeking to escape the death penalty through a federal writ of habeas corpus.

The writ of habeas corpus is ancient, powerful, and enshrined in the Constitution of the United States. Literally, it means "show the body," and in modern America it represents the ability of a prisoner to file a civil suit against his or her imprisoner, asking to be released or (in the case of the death penalty) to be freed from a wrongful sentence. Thus, if the police arrest the wrong person, that prisoner can sue for a writ of habeas corpus; if a woman is held without a charge, she can file such a suit; and those on death row can petition for a writ of habeas corpus to challenge their pending execution as unlawful.

Federal law and the law of the many states contain provisions for habeas corpus, but the most important form of habeas is probably federal review of a state prisoner's case. Because of the availability of federal habeas corpus procedures, someone held by state authorities has the ability to have her or his case reviewed by someone not employed by that state. As Eric M. Freedman has written, "This system of dual safeguards makes sense, implementing the fundamental, and mutually consistent, conceptions of individual liberty and constrained government power that underlie the Constitution."[1]

How ancient is habeas corpus? Some commentators trace it back before the Magna Carta in English common law, and that common law served as the basis for the law of the American colonies. One popular treatise makes this connection quite graphically:

> The ultimate threads have not been traced but within a century after the victory of William in 1066 when the population of the world did not much exceed that of the United States today, and the "blessed plot" now known as England consisted of a small tribe of rude men still eating with their hands, the writ of habeas corpus was in general use.[2]

By the time the newborn United States was framing its Constitution, the writ of habeas corpus was already an old and familiar part of the common law. That may account for the somewhat offhand way that the writ is provided for in the Constitution. Rather than guarantee the right to petition for habeas corpus, the Constitution instead establishes limits on when that right can be suspended in an emergency. The suspension clause of the Constitution's article 1, section 9 provides that "the Privilege of the Writ of Habeas Corpus shall not be suspended, unless when in Cases of Rebellion or Invasion the public Safety may require it." Perhaps the idea of habeas is all the more powerful in that the

Constitution, rather than defining it, simply assumes that it exists. At any rate, the extraordinary nature of habeas corpus, by which one sovereign (the federal government) can free or keep alive the prisoner of another sovereign (the state) is significant enough that it is often referred to within the world of law as the *Great Writ*.

Every day, state prisoners file habeas petitions in federal courts. If their case is accepted, they are sent from the state system to the federal system for further consideration, much as Jesus was shuttled from Pilate to Herod for the same purpose.

It is impossible to know the exact relationship between Pilate and Herod, but it does seem clear that they represented different sorts of authority. Of the several Herods mentioned in the Bible, experts think the Herod mentioned here is Herod Antipas, who was the ruler of Galilee until A.D. 39, when Emperor Caligula exiled him to Lyons in present-day France.[3] While views differ on the authority of Herod Antipas, it seems that the Romans gave him power to rule Galilee. Thus, he was not a king, but a ruler who had similar powers to those of Pilate under Rome, covering a different geographic area. As Raymond Brown put it, "In his own territory the tetrarch Herod's powers would not be much different from Pilate's powers as prefect in Judea and Samaria."[4]

If that's true, it appears that Pilate heard Jesus' appeal, then realized that he was from the area controlled by Herod. Since Herod was in town for the festival, Pilate sent Jesus to Herod because Pilate wanted "an independent evaluation from someone who had a legal relationship to Jesus."[5] While the geographic division of authority does not track the way habeas works, in a more general way there is an analogy to be made: after an appeal, a separate authority was allowed to review the case and opine, in a way that foreshadows our modern practice.

Herod and Jesus were known to each other. Luke reported that as Jesus headed to Jerusalem—but before he got there—he was warned that Herod was out to get him and he sent a message back to the ruler:

> At that very hour some Pharisees came and said to him, "Get away from here, for Herod wants to kill you." He said to them,

"Go and tell that fox for me, 'Listen, I am casting out demons and performing cures today and tomorrow, and on the third day I finish my work.'" (Luke 13:31-32)

One would think that this bit of taunting probably made Jesus more an object of interest to Herod, who must have been surprised to find that same Jesus delivered to him as a prisoner in Jerusalem. Once Jesus was turned over, we know that Herod was "very glad, for he had been wanting to see him for a long time" (Luke 23:8). Herod took time to review the case, while the chief priests made their accusations (Luke 23:10).

In the end, Herod mocked Jesus and sent him back to Pilate. Remember, that (within Luke's description, anyway) came after Pilate decided that there was "no basis for an accusation" against Jesus (Luke 23:4). Jesus gave Herod no reason to think differently, and there didn't appear to be anything new in the arguments of the chief priests. Yet Herod sent Jesus back to be executed.

Within the context of modern law, given these facts we would say that Jesus had a very high burden before Herod. That is, if Jesus was to be freed, he would have had to convince Herod of an extreme injustice. In this respect, at least, we have a very direct parallel to our present system of federal habeas review of state capital cases.

In 1996, President Bill Clinton signed into law a new and complex set of laws that made habeas much tougher for those on death row. That law, the Antiterrorism and Effective Death Penalty Act, is usually known by the unwieldy moniker of the AEDPA. This law, like many others in the field of criminal law, was perhaps enacted more as a reaction to a particular event than a well-considered and debated proposal from Congress (another example is the imposition of stiff crack cocaine penalties in the wake of the cocaine-related death of basketball player Len Bias). Though some in Washington, including Chief Justice William Rehnquist, had sought tougher restrictions on habeas for some time, the political moment for passage of these reforms was provided by Oklahoma City federal building bomber Timothy McVeigh. In 1996, an election year, McVeigh was on death row, and many feared he would evade execution through the extensive filing of habeas petitions. In part because of this political motive, habeas was restricted.[6]

One of those changes imposed a standard, much like that Jesus seemed to face, on habeas petitioners. Where a state prisoner is seeking habeas relief in federal courts, the following standard applies under 28 U.S. Code §2254(e)(1):

> In a proceeding instituted by an application for a writ of habeas corpus by a person in custody pursuant to the judgment of a state court, a determination of a factual issue made by a state court shall be presumed to be correct. The applicant shall have the burden of rebutting the presumption of correctness by clear and convincing evidence.

Thus, like Jesus, the prisoner who is presented to a new authority to argue for freedom has a tough task; the decision below is presumed to be correct. Moreover, it is not enough to prove that the decision below is probably wrong; rather, the prisoner has to prove that the lower court was wrong by clear and convincing evidence, a burden much higher than is usually faced in other federal civil actions.

Nor is this the only impediment to habeas created, enhanced, or retained by the AEDPA. Federal habeas law now imposes a one-year time limit after appeal to file for a writ;[7] requires that all possible state remedies be exhausted before filing for habeas in federal court;[8] allows only for review of a violation of "clearly established Federal law," thus barring the development of new law;[9] and must include all issues in one petition unless special dispensation is given by a federal court of appeals.[10]

As a graduate of Yale Law School, a practitioner in the federal courts for fifteen years, and a professor who teaches appellate and habeas procedures, I find this welter of restrictions hopelessly confusing. I cannot resolve even seemingly simple issues without resorting to research on the case law, statute, and commentary, and even then I am not sure of the answer. It is, without a doubt, the most confusing and poorly defined area of law in which I practice.

Nevertheless, those who bring these petitions often don't have so much as a high-school education, and they have only limited access to law books and no access to supposed experts. Despite these daunting complexities, most petitions on habeas are brought by the prisoners themselves. Like Jesus before Herod, the prisoner stands alone.

It is a particularly harsh match—the least educated practitioners engaging the most complex area of criminal law. Prisoners, especially for the most serious crimes, are rarely people who have been successful in school. For example, when Florida tested prisoners using the Test of Adult Basic Education, it found that the average prisoner had the educational equivalent of a fifth or sixth grader.[11]

Moreover, prisoners filing habeas petitions rarely have attorneys to help them. One Florida prisoner and jailhouse lawyer, Thomas C. O'Bryant, claimed, "In nearly eleven years of incarceration, I have never seen, nor heard of, a non–death row prisoner having a court-appointed or pro bono attorney research, draft, and file post-conviction pleadings for him."[12] O'Bryant's observation shouldn't be surprising, since few inmates would be able to afford an attorney, and there is no general right to a court-appointed attorney to help with habeas appeals.

Of course, an incarcerated man is not likely to have many resources at his disposal to help make sense of the restrictions on habeas. Certainly, the books available in a prison library are going to be limited, sometimes to little more than the statutes and a case reporter.[13] There are even obstacles to the prisoners helping one another. O'Bryant notes that inmates are often barred from possessing the legal papers of another prisoner, making such assistance especially difficult.[14]

Herod could have freed Jesus, but chose not to. In our world, this decision is often not so straightforward; the question too often gets mired in procedure rather than a discussion of truth or examination of the real problems with a conviction or sentence. It could be that not only do we embrace the outcome chosen by Herod, but that we get to it through indirection and a hopelessly confusing process.

The Governor Denies Clemency

Now at the festival the governor was accustomed to release a prisoner for the crowd, anyone whom they wanted. At that time they had a notorious prisoner, called Jesus Barabbas. So after they had gathered, Pilate said to them, "Whom do you want me to release for you, Jesus Barabbas or Jesus who is called the Messiah?" For he realized that it was out of jealousy that they had handed him over. While he was sitting on his judgment seat, his wife sent word to him, "Have nothing to do with that innocent man, for today I have suffered a great deal because of a dream about him." Now the chief priests and the elders persuaded the crowds to ask for Barabbas and to have Jesus killed. The governor again said to them, "Which of the two do you want me to release for you?" And they said, "Barabbas."   —Matthew 27:15-21

Pilate, like the governors of American states today, apparently had the power to grant clemency, but he bowed to political pressure and declined to commute the death sentence already given to Jesus. Even down to the last moments of legal process, then, Jesus' path seemed to be an accelerated version of the route taken by modern capital cases, in which the final attempt to save the life of the defendant is very often a request for commutation of the death sentence to the governor of the sentencing state. Even the complexities that arise in this well-known story have modern analogues, including the political pressures felt by the governor and the role of the chief priests and elders in the role of advisers to the governor.

Executive clemency can be expressed one of two ways—either by a governor *pardoning* the prisoner or by a governor *commuting* his or her sentence. Historically, pardoning has the effect of nullifying the conviction; the Supreme Court once said that it "blots out the offence."[1] Commutation of a death sentence, on the other hand, simply changes the sentence while the conviction remains. In a death penalty case, once a death sentence is commuted, the defendant most often is going to serve a life sentence in prison.

The ability of a governor to grant clemency is an anomaly in the realm of criminal law. Clemency essentially allows one man or woman to undo the rulings of a jury and (usually) several courts that have already reviewed the case. In that sense, it is in conflict with an ordered justice system in that it upends both the established law and the process that has uniformly affirmed that law up that point. As such, it perhaps can best be called an expression of mercy by the governor.

Clemency is an ancient power of the executive, brought to the United States from the British legal system. The United States Constitution, article 2, section 2, expressly grants the president the power to give pardons and reprieves, and state constitutions give governors the same power.

The history of clemency in Texas is especially intriguing. The governor's power to grant clemency is included in the Texas Constitution,[2] and it has been a constitutional prerogative of the governor since Texas became a state in 1845. However, in the early part of the twentieth century, a series of governors were particularly profligate with the power to forgive—in just two years (1915–1917), Governor James E. Ferguson exercised clemency more than two thousand times, and his successors W. P. Hobby (1917–1921) and Miriam A. Ferguson (1925–1927) each used the power more than one thousand times. As a result, the state constitution was amended so that the governor's power to use clemency was limited by the new requirement that he or she first receive a majority vote of the Board of Pardons and Paroles in support of that action.[3] Other states have created such boards to advise the governor, to restrain him or her (as in Texas), or in some cases, to take over the entire clemency responsibilities.[4]

The effect of this change was not as dramatic as one might think. Until 1972 (when the Supreme Court struck down Texas's death penalty scheme in *Furman v. Georgia*), about 20 percent of those on death row received clemency. The dramatic change happened only *after* the death penalty was revived in Texas in 1976. Since that time, more than 360 prisoners have been executed, nearly all of whom sought commutation, but only one received a grant of clemency.[5] Effectively, clemency no longer exists on death row in Texas. The reason may be that once the death penalty returned, it was an even more significant political issue because the entire institution of capital punishment was under threat. After that point, given the pro–death penalty beliefs of the Texas electorate, if one wanted to become or remain the governor of Texas, strict support of capital punishment became a political necessity.

Despite the fact that clemency functionally no longer operates in the state with the most executions, Texas, clemency is still held out by the United States Supreme Court as an essential part of the system of capital punishment review. Indeed, clemency is seen as a sort of fail-safe measure that allows other parts of the process to turn away from some issues. Perhaps most notably, in the 1993 case of *Herrera v. Collins*,[6] the Supreme Court said that a person on death row should not be set free on a writ of habeas corpus simply because new evidence shows him or her to be innocent.[7] Though many readers considered that portion of the opinion not part of the holding of the court, the idea that evidence of innocence could be so easily dismissed shocked many observers because of its seeming indifference to the problem of executing innocent defendants. To mitigate this worry, the majority opinion (written by Chief Justice Rehnquist) emphasized that the petitioner still had the ability to ask the governor for commutation of his sentence:

This is not to say, however, that petitioner is left without a forum to raise his actual innocence claim. For under Texas law, petitioner may file a request for executive clemency. Clemency is deeply rooted in our Anglo-American tradition of law, and is the historic remedy for preventing miscarriages of justice where judicial process has been exhausted.[8]

Thus, the Supreme Court shunted off the question of whether a possibly innocent man may be executed to the governor of Texas, through the exercise of clemency. Sadly, then, at the same time that the appellate courts were effectively deregulating the states' death penalty processes, the Texas governors that the Supreme Court was counting on to carefully consider each case were becoming monolithic in their rejection of commutation requests. What Whit Cobb wrote in 1989 holds even more true today:

Max Weber, then, was right: the impassive, rationalistic impulse of bureaucracy is inexorable, even in death. The element of mercy is being squeezed out of capital punishment in the United States by a death penalty bureaucracy.[9]

And what of mercy, then? For Christians, the idea of executive clemency is particularly important in that it represents one point in the process where true mercy can be shown. Jurors, after all, may be expressly instructed that they are to ignore "mere sentiment, conjecture, sympathy, passion, prejudice, public opinion, or public feeling."[10] Trial judges, understandably, are loath to reverse the decision of a jury, and in all capital cases it is the jury, not the judge, who is going to determine the sentence. In turn, the task of appellate judges is to articulate more universal themes of law that will then apply broadly, and rarely is there a chance for them to express mercy as part of their rulings. The clemency decision of the governor is the last and best hope for an expression of mercy.

Early on in the history of the United States, there seems to have been an express recognition that mercy was a part of the power to commute sentences. In 1833, the Supreme Court described the ability of the executive to pardon defendants as "an act of grace."[11] Over time, however, this attitude has eroded. By 1927, the

Supreme Court had seemingly changed its mind, saying, "A pardon in our days is not a private act of grace from an individual happening to possess power. It is part of the Constitutional scheme."[12] Still, the possibility for decisions based on mercy remains into the present day; even in those states with parole and pardon boards that influence decisions, they usually lack uniform standards by which to make their decisions, and once those decisions are made, federal courts usually seem to treat them as beyond review and wholly within the discretion of the executive.[13] Except for the political repercussions, there is not much keeping governors and parole boards from employing mercy now and then, but the political effects of doing so in a place like Texas can be significant.

In keeping with this shift, state governors (with the exception of Illinois' Governor George Ryan) don't do much in the way of mercy these days; rather, most seem to view commutation of death sentences the same way that Bill Clinton did in his second term as governor of Arkansas. In his first term, Clinton commuted several death sentences, and he believed that was one reason he was not reelected. After a few years out of office, Clinton campaigned for a second term as governor on the promise not to commute sentences so liberally, and he defined that process in a way that systemically excluded mercy: "The appeals process, though lengthy, provides many opportunities for the courts to review sentences and that's where these decisions should be made."[14] In other words, if the law is followed (and this is confirmed by the appellate courts), there should be no chance for mercy. Clinton knows the Bible, but perhaps he did not think of the parallels between the person he had become and the chief priests who urged Pilate to complete the execution because the law had been followed. When Pilate told them that he might release Jesus, they replied, "We have a law, and according to that law he ought to die" (John 19:7).

Clinton was hardly alone in fearing the political consequences of showing mercy to those on death row, and he had only to look to the experience of other future presidents to see the importance of the issue. In 1966, Ronald Reagan was elected governor of California over Pat Brown, who believed that he lost because he had granted clemency to some of those on death row.[15] In red-state America, the support for the death penalty expressed by political candidates can get downright silly; one candidate for the Texas Supreme Court even advertised her enthusiasm for capital punishment. The problem with her advertisement was that Texas has not one but two supreme courts, one for criminal matters and one for civil appeals. The Court of Criminal Appeals, not the Supreme Court, has jurisdiction over capital appeals.[16]

Right up to the minute, in Texas at least, political pressures cause those in a position to allow mercy into the system to flinch at the idea. They are, of course, the modern-day echoes of Pilate, for whom the political pressure was very immediate—there was a crowd before him chanting for death. There is one crucial difference, however: due to the festival tradition, one of the condemned, Jesus Barabbas or Jesus Christ, was going to go free. One or the other was to receive mercy, an arrangement never seen in Texas.

Barabbas was in some ways the mirror image of Christ. While both sought the overthrow of worldly empires, Christ sought change through nonviolence and transcendence; Barabbas was a more traditional rebel. Mark told us that Barabbas was among the "rebels who had committed murder during the insurrection" (15:7). While Christ was threatening to the priests, especially when he overturned the money changers' tables at the temple, he was not the kind of direct threat to Rome that a rebel like Barabbas would represent. If one of them had to go, you would think it would be an easy call for the emissary of Rome: release the preacher who rode in on a donkey, and kill the rebel who with his band of confederates had already shown the willingness to kill in their quest for power. It certainly seems that Pilate had the power to do so; after all, he was the Roman authority in a Roman province, and the people yelling at him were subjects he could have crushed, not voters. Yet in response to the cries of the crowd (and the urging of the chief priests, who perhaps can be seen to take on the role of an ad hoc Board of Pardons and Paroles), he released the rebel, whose actions foreshadowed the much more significant rebellion that would consume Jerusalem from A.D. 66 to 70. Even though he suspected that

Jesus was innocent, even though his wife urged him to free Jesus Christ, even though it meant releasing a murdering rebel against Rome, Pilate responded to the crowd. Though the members of that crowd were neither his peers nor those who would elect him, Pilate seemed to share the weakness of many politicians—the desire to be liked overwhelms any principles once the hard decisions must be made.

Though no one seems to know the origins of the festival tradition of releasing a prisoner, theologian Raymond Brown notes that official procedure would have been in flux at that time as Rome switched from being a republic to an empire.[17] By Brown's analysis, the festival tradition best fits the Roman term *venia*, which could be "extended independently of guilt—indeed to one known to be guilty."[18] Thus, it could be an expression of pure unearned mercy, untainted by questions of possible innocence, and it seems to be exactly the sort of undeserved mercy that Jesus Barabbas, the rebel, received.

Victoria J. Palacios slings a well-placed rock in condemning the decay of commutation in capital cases in the United States, accurately describing our process as one in which "many people play a small role in death decisions, no one takes sole, personal responsibility for the decision, and the final decision makers are subject to strong political pressure."[19] This stinging rebuke, however, is hardly new. Perhaps its entire essence is summed up in one of the most enduring images in the Bible, that of Pilate, once the request for clemency had been denied, washing his hands of it before the crowd (Matt 27:24). The symbolism is clear; Pilate stood before the washbasin imagining he bore no responsibility for the death of Jesus Christ because a process had been followed. In the present day, it seems there is a limitless supply of washbasins in the governor's mansion in Austin and in governors' mansions across the South.

CHAPTER FOURTEEN

HUMILIATION OF THE CONVICTED

Then the soldiers of the governor took Jesus into the governor's headquarters, and they gathered the whole cohort around him. They stripped him and put a scarlet robe on him, and after twisting some thorns into a crown, they put it on his head. They put a reed in his right hand and knelt before him and mocked him, saying, "Hail, King of the Jews!" They spat on him, and took the reed and struck him on the head. —Matthew 27:27-30

Many of the most public and replicated images of Christ are those showing his humiliation in the course of his punishment: the figure on the cross dying in public, the crown of thorns, the carrying of the cross to the execution. Mel Gibson's entire film *The Passion of the Christ* focused principally on the pain and humiliation of Christ. While the use of humiliation as punishment in the passion story may seem extralegal, once again his path crosses with the controversies of modern criminal law. The use and role of humiliation as punishment, including some of the same punishments inflicted on Christ, are now a hot topic among jurists and academics, and over the past several years some judges have started to revive the old tradition of using humiliation as a sentencing tool. As in the other areas of the law, a reflection upon the experience of Christ may illuminate this modern debate.

Certainly, there is no lack of humiliations of Christ to discuss. One remarkable aspect of the story of Christ's punishment is that so *many* people played a role in the humiliations over the course of just one day. It seems that each stage of the process after conviction (except the first appearance before Pilate) included an aspect of humiliation, beginning nearly the moment he was convicted. That he endured these punishments and emerged to victory defines Christ; perhaps the fact that we mortals can inflict such humiliations should serve as a warning about our worst impulses.

First, immediately after the council condemned him, Jesus was mocked and belittled. Apparently while he was still in the chamber where the trial was held, some of those present began to spit on him and then grew even crueler. Blindfolding him, they took turns hitting him, then goaded him to "prophesy" who had struck him (Mark 14:65).[1] As with the later episodes of humiliation, it was not random behavior; rather, it was cruelty specifically linked to the charges against him and his role as a prophet, making it seem more like a form of punishment than an idle game played by mindless guards.

When Jesus first appeared before Pilate, the governor in his amazement did not mock or humiliate the prisoner; at least none of the Gospels reported additional cruelties at that point. It was, though, a brief respite. Herod, whom Luke said reviewed the case after the first appearance before Pilate, did not miss the opportunity to get in his licks. Luke reported that "Herod with his soldiers treated him with contempt and mocked him; then he put an elegant robe on him and sent him back to Pilate" (Luke 23:11). The robe, of course, was an intentional choice designed to mock Jesus for the crime he was said to have committed—the claim of being a king.

When Jesus was returned to the governor once Herod was finished with him, Pilate did not pass up a second chance to interject some public humiliation into the process. After he deferred to the will of the crowd and freed Barabbas, Pilate proceeded to flog Jesus before the crowd. Mark reported that in an almost offhand way: "So Pilate, wishing to satisfy the crowd, released Barabbas for them; and after flogging Jesus, he handed him over to be crucified" (15:15).

The flogging seemed to be an afterthought and was doubly humiliating in that Jesus was not then going to be freed, but killed.

After the flogging by Pilate, the soldiers humiliated Jesus by dressing him up as a king, with a purple cloak and a crown of thorns. The use of the color purple had a definite meaning—purple dye was expensive, and probably was used only for royal attire. At the grand funeral for Herod the Great, for example, the body was wrapped in purple.[2] Purple was the color of kings. Once the soldiers had dressed Jesus up as royalty, they pretended to kneel down in homage to him (Mark 15:16-18). It seemed almost unspeakably cruel, given that Jesus was on his way to death, but again it was not random; rather, it furthered the punishment for the crime and was a strikingly specific cruelty.

The cruelty of the soldiers, relative to the other humiliations, seemed to be the taunting of individual bullies rather than an act of the justice system. It was also more personal in a way—being forced to appear in the robe of a king at the height of a very public experience, an appearance that cut against every humble moment that Christ had exhibited in his time on earth. Like a convict today who is taunted or hit as he picks up trash by the highway, Jesus was not only subjected to the mechanized humiliations of a process, but was also made available for the random cruel acts of individuals who might enjoy the opportunity.

Nor were the cruel acts of the soldiers the end of Christ's shaming. Even on the way to the place of death, Jesus might have been made to carry his own cross (John 19:17) before Simon of Cyrene, a bystander, was recruited to take over (Mark 15:21).[3] It was Roman custom to have the condemned man carry the heavy horizontal bar of a cross to the place of execution, where the vertical bar was permanently positioned in the ground. Some experts have deduced that having Simon carry the bar was not an act of kindness, but that Jesus had simply become too weak to carry the bar any farther.[4] This tradition, of having the condemned man do the work for his own execution, would be akin to making the modern prisoner inject himself with the deadly drugs or generate the electricity for his electrocution. It also was a particularly public humiliation; Jesus had to travel on the road with the device of his death as "a great number of the people followed him" (Luke 23:27).

The choice of a public, and slow, method of death such as crucifixion certainly heightened the humiliating aspects of the execution of Jesus, but further intentional steps were taken by those who had condemned him. While Jesus was on the cross, dying, they taunted him with the charge of his conviction, yelling, "Let him save himself if he is the Messiah of God!" (Luke 23:35). Even one of the criminals hanging beside Jesus joined in this taunting (Luke 23:39).

The final jab of humiliation was the sign they posted over Jesus' head, reading "King of the Jews" (Luke 23:38). Roman authors of the time described the practice of using such a *titulus* as a method of humiliation. It would label the charge against the defendant and would sometimes be hung around the neck of the condemned man as he died.[5]

We do none of these things as a part of the modern execution process. There is no direct corollary to our procedures because we do not force condemned people to put up with any of the things that Jesus experienced. However, while our executions certainly reflect much more of an effort to preserve the dignity of condemned people than was allowed by the Romans, there still are calls for more humiliation and even torture to be a part of the death penalty process, and certainly voices that call for a more public form of execution. For example, punishment expert Austin Sarat has called for executions to be televised so that the mechanics of the death penalty can be thoroughly understood.[6] While televised executions are unlikely to become a reality, in the past few decades we have taken one step toward a more public form of execution by allowing the families of victims to attend executions in some states.[7]

In noncapital cases, meanwhile, courts have begun to experiment with punishments employing humiliation. Strikingly, a large number of these employ one of the primary methods used against Christ—the old Roman trick of placing a sign publicly identifying the offense on the convict as he was punished. For example, two defendants in Ohio, Jessica Lange and Brian Patrick, were convicted in 2003 of defacing a statue of Jesus. The judge who sentenced them chose a punishment of pure humiliation: the couple was forced to walk a donkey through the streets of Fairport Harbor, Ohio, while holding a sign saying, "Sorry for the jackass offense."[8]

Similarly, a Florida judge forced a thief to hold a sign saying, "I am a convicted thief," and another defendant (presumably, not a pharmacist) to display one saying, "Selling prescription drugs is a crime; I'm a felon because I sold prescription drugs." In Illinois, a man was ordered to put a sign on his lawn reading, "Warning! A violent felon lives here. Enter at your own risk!" Meanwhile those who solicit prostitutes may end up with their picture on a ten-by-twenty-foot billboard (in Oakland) or have their picture broadcast on cable television (in Kansas City). Perhaps most creatively, a judge in Ohio sentenced a defendant who called a police officer a "pig" to stand in a pigpen (complete with a live pig) while displaying a sign saying, "This is not a police officer."[9]

Even the relatively liberal United States Ninth Circuit Court of Appeals has upheld a sentence that relied on shaming in addition to a two-month sentence of incarceration. There, a man convicted of theft from the mail was told to stand outside the post office and carry a sandwich board announcing, "I stole mail. This is my punishment."[10]

Shaming punishments, of course, are nothing new to American law. A popular feature of Colonial Williamsburg is the set of colonial-era stocks near the middle of town, where tourists can have their pictures taken while their head and hands are trapped between two boards with appropriate-sized holes. Their original purpose, of course, was a punishment that had more to do with humiliation than confinement. Convicts were placed in the stocks to be mocked by passersby, and at the least displayed in public for their misdeeds, perhaps with a sign describing the crime.

The return of shaming punishments to American criminal law has been encouraged by some academics, including Yale Law professor Dan M. Kahan, who wrote an influential article in 1996 that promoted the use of shaming sanctions as a politically acceptable alternative to imprisonment.[11] Though Kahan later recanted his support of shaming as a form of sentencing,[12] his work not only coincided with an emboldened use of humiliation in sentencing, but also helped begin an active debate over the practice.

One aspect of this debate was an examination of the reasons we would want to humiliate a defendant in the first place. Certainly, it is punishment, and we have consensus in this country that it is acceptable to punish criminals, but why *that* form of punishment? It seems to reflect a form of inner rage, a frustration with the inability to control the actions of offenders who do dumb and destructive things and will not stop. For example, the mail thief in the sandwich board, Shawn Gementera, who had already been convicted of criminal mischief, battery, and possession of drug paraphernalia, was only twenty-four years old.[13] Presumably, other punishments had not worked.

While the modern shaming punishments described above were for crimes that are trivial compared to those committed by the murderers on death row, the motivations for using shaming and humiliation are probably the same as those that led the Roman authorities to humiliate Christ. One such motivation was to deter others from committing similar acts, a message broadcast by the sign over the dying body of Christ just as clearly as the mail thief trudging through the crowds in his sandwich board. In fact, one can imagine that one of the bandits executed on either side of Christ displayed a similar sign decrying his theft.

Another motivation was to enhance the punishment value of the sentence—a jail sentence for a minor crime may last for just a few days and be served out in relative privacy, but the effects of such an episode of sentencing by humiliation may last for a lifetime, especially in a small community.

There may be a deeper motivation as well, that which compels us to dehumanize defendants so that we can punish them without guilt. Psychologist Sharon Lamb, looking at this legal debate from the perspective of her expertise, started her analysis from the observation that "all agree that the emotion of disgust may be a prime motivator, sometimes appropriate and sometimes not, of condemnation."[14] Examining condemnation as expressed through shaming sanctions, Lamb describes the need to isolate and dehumanize the defendant so that he or she can be punished properly with an appropriate air of disgust: "The urge to condemn in these cases goes hand-in-hand with seeing the wrongdoer as less of a person."[15]

Lamb's observation certainly makes sense when we consider both modern shaming and the humiliation of Christ. In the modern example, it is necessary to isolate and shame the defendant because the crime hits so close to our own impulses. As Lamb puts it, we demonize sex offenders, for example, because in a culture awash in sexual imagery, sex offenders "evoke a fear of our own sexuality, a fear that it will spiral out of control or that it can be disgusting and misplaced."[16] That is, the public demonizing is necessary to place the offender in the realm of disgust rather than titillation, which defines much of the rest of our society. Similarly, many people have the impulse to steal little things or deface something, but resist; that common impulse may explain the very public condemnation of petty thieves and vandals described above. When we mock them, we define their acts as distinct from impulses we may feel.

In the ancient example of Christ's humiliation, though, we are looking at something very different. Christ's "crime" was not one that we imagine or are tempted by; rather, it is inconceivable to those who view him as the Son of God. Only insane people, in fact, imagine that they have the powers of Christ. Given that he was accused of something far bigger than those petty temptations we feel, the need to dehumanize and degrade him came from somewhere else—from the need to make him seem like just another man in order to debunk his claims. Those who thought they had brought him low, of course, did not see the rebuke of Easter coming.

So what does the story of Christ's humiliations offer us in relation to the modern criminal law? In part, confronting the cruelties visited on Christ might expose the cruel impulses that lie behind the shaming of any defendant, including those convicted of relatively petty crimes. Whatever the purpose for dehumanizing the persons who have wronged society, perhaps it is beneath us to give in to that impulse and hang a sign around their neck describing their crimes as they are paraded down the street. That we would stoop to the tactics employed in capital cases by the ancient Romans to punish petty crimes may well show how broken and base our system of punishments truly has become.

The Gospels tell the story not only of Christ but also of those around him, such as the Roman soldiers and their purple robe. We learn of the divine humility of Christ and of the utter inability of the mortal accusers to successfully use humiliation as a tool. Sophisticated as we are, we may still lack the power to fully know, understand, and use the power of public humiliation, which not only relies on a complex understanding of human nature but also requires an utter certainty of guilt if such psychological damage is to be reasonably inflicted, especially for minor crimes. Two thousand years later, it is clear that Christ's tormentors truly knew not what they were doing, and there is little basis for the belief that human nature has changed in some profound way in the interim.

CHAPTER FIFTEEN

A CRUEL AND UNUSUAL EXECUTION

Then they brought Jesus to the place called Golgotha (which means the place of a skull). And they offered him wine mixed with myrrh; but he did not take it. And they crucified him. —Mark 15:22-24

The symbol of Christianity is nothing less than the device of execution used to crush the body of the Savior. This is fitting—the crucifixion of Christ is part of what makes the story of the Gospels so compelling; its cruelty repulses us and heightens (for Christians) the nature of the victory that follows. Some commentators have even called the device of crucifixion, the simple cross, "a form of Roman imperial terrorism."[1]

Although something so vile as crucifixion is no longer used as a means of execution, the story of Christ's killing bears certain parallels to the use of lethal injection as a means of execution in the United States. Intriguingly, the form of lethal injection used by most states replicates, through chemical means, the three known steps of Christ's execution. Those three steps, in both the ancient and the modern methods, are first to administer anesthesia; second to disable and restrain the body; and third to kill the body.

In the modern variation on this process, pharmaceuticals are used: first a medical anesthetic is administered, then a second chemical is injected to paralyze the body, and finally a lethal dosage of a third chemical causes death. In the execution of Christ these same steps were followed: anesthesia was offered (the wine and myrrh), the condemned man was disabled (nailed to the cross), and death was caused (as the cross was assembled and Christ left there without a way to support his body).

The three-drug execution cocktail used in American capital punishment has repeatedly come under scrutiny. Though the Supreme Court has approved this process as used in Kentucky, it did so over the dissent of two justices and while expressing concern about the method. That opinion, in *Baze v. Rees*, held that a method of execution is unconstitutional only if it "creates a demonstrated risk of severe pain,"[2] a standard that some feel will require constant reexamination of execution methods. Once again, the example of Christ proves to be more relevant to a current issue in criminal law than one might guess.

The actual death of Christ is discussed only briefly in the Gospels. We do know, if we believe the words of Mark, that Jesus was offered wine mixed with another substance (which he refused [15:23]), that he was attached to the cross and crucified (15:24), that he suffered such pain that he wondered whether God had forsaken him (15:34), and that he died as a result of the crucifixion (15:37). These facts, though, are enough to track the steps of his execution.

According to Mark, before Jesus was put on the cross, he was offered wine mixed with myrrh (15:23).[3] Wine, in itself, was described in the Old Testament as a way to numb pain. Proverbs 31:6 instructs, "Give strong drink to one who is perishing, / and wine to those in bitter distress." In keeping with this admonition (intentionally or not), Jesus was offered wine not only before the crucifixion but also while he hung on the cross (Mark 15:36).

What makes the story more interesting (and more relevant to the modern debate over lethal injection) is the report that Jesus was offered not just wine, but wine mixed with myrrh. In one sense, this provides a bookend to the earthly life of Jesus, since myrrh was one of the gifts presented to the baby Jesus by the wise men, who came to visit him shortly after his birth (Matt 2:11). On a more practical level, though, the myrrh might have been added to heighten the anesthetic effect of the wine. Though little is known about the use of myrrh for this purpose in ancient times,[4] biblical scholar Raymond Brown notes, "Passages in later Jewish writings attest to the offering of scented wine to the condemned as an anesthetic."[5]

The second step, disabling the condemned person, is achieved chemically in the modern era but mechanically in the crucifixion. None of the Gospel accounts described whether Jesus was nailed or tied to the cross, but reports of the risen Christ included a description of wounds to the hands (Luke 24:39; John 20:25, 27). In perhaps the crudest way imaginable, nailing a man to a wooden beam achieves the goal of incapacitating him so that he cannot resist or escape once the throes of death begin.

The final step of the crucifixion, death, was achieved by attaching the crossbeam to the vertical part of the cross and leaving him on the cross once the cross was fully assembled and the body of the prisoner was fully lifted above the ground. Practically, it would be nearly impossible to nail someone to a cross after the horizontal beam was attached, especially if that horizontal beam was some seven feet in the air.[6] The disabling of the condemned person was probably performed by nailing him to the crossbar; in turn, the cause of death would be lifting that crossbar into place and leaving Jesus there to perish.

Over the centuries, the specifics of *how* crucifixion caused death have been the object of some speculation in the medical community. Of course, medical studies on it cannot be ethically conducted, though the Nazis may have conducted experiments on crucifixion at Dachau.[7] In the 1800s, some doctors speculated that the effect of the crucifixion was to rupture Jesus' heart. Such a cause of death would fulfill part of the prophecy of Psalm 22, which foreshadowed many aspects of Jesus' death as described in the Gospels. Specifically, Psalm 22 contains the lament of a dying man: "My heart is like wax; / it is melted within my breast" (v. 14).

Others have held that Jesus would have died of dehydration and loss of blood. The general consensus, though, as described in 1986 by Dr. W. D. Edwards of the Mayo Clinic, seems to be that crucifixion caused death by interfering with breathing as a condemned man slumped downward under his own weight, causing death by asphyxiation.[8]

A fair guess at the events of crucifixion would include the offering of anesthesia, the disabling of Christ, and then the killing of Christ by painful asphyxiation, dehydration, or a rupture of the heart. With that background in mind, let us now consider the modern controversy around lethal injections, which at one point led thirteen states to put executions on hold.[9] At the center of that controversy is the controversial three-step chemical regimen that seeks to anesthetize, disable, then kill a prisoner.

Lethal injection is a fairly recent phenomenon, coming at the tail end of decades spent seeking an acceptable manner of execution. If nothing else, the experience of execution in the United States has repeatedly proved that there is no easy way to kill a person. The human body, it seems, resists death by hanging, electrocution, gas, and chemical injection, leaving no clean and tidy options for the executioner.

In the early years of the republic, hanging was the preferred method of killing prisoners. However, that was often problematic. New York State suffered a series of botched hangings in the early 1800s, and the mistakes were made in full view of the several thousand people who attended these spectacles. Finally, in 1885, the governor of New York commissioned a committee to study alternatives to hanging. After a lengthy period of study, this committee recommended the first use of an electric chair, and New York strove for reform by changing to that method.[10]

Electrocution, though, did not prove to be much of an improvement. The first person seated in New York's new electric chair was a murderer named William Kemmler. Rather than being neatly dispatched, however, Kemmler did not die quickly, and he slowly expired amidst the smell of burning flesh and ashes.[11] For more than one hundred years, the electric chair was used with varying results. In 1999, Allen Lee Davis was executed by electrocution in Florida—poorly. During the execution, he was badly burned and left bleeding. Gory photos of the execution were posted on the Florida Supreme Court's website, and so many people tried to see them that the system crashed and was disabled for months.

Until fairly recently, a wide variety of execution methods was used, each presenting its own problems. Firing squads could misfire, the electric chair offered wildly uneven results, and by the estimation of execution expert Deborah Denno, the gas chamber was the worst of them all. Speaking of an execution in Arizona, Denno recalls that "Donald Harding's eleven-minute execution and suffocating pain were so disturbing for witnesses that reporters cried, the attorney general vomited, and the prison warden claimed he would resign if forced to conduct another lethal gas execution."[12]

Out of these many problematic procedures came a general consensus that lethal injection is the best possible choice. In the United States, every state with the death penalty except Nebraska has made lethal injection the default method of execution, though some states allow the condemned person to choose an alternative method. The reasons for this consensus are unclear, but one reason might be the perception that lethal injection is the most humane of the possible options.[13] Part of that perception might draw from the fact that the lethal injection method, unlike hanging, the electric chair, or lethal gas, resembles a therapeutic use of medicine. This is especially true since the sedative and (particularly) the paralyzing agent often prevent the prisoner from screaming or thrashing around during the execution.

Given the seeming agreement that lethal injection is the best choice for executions, one would expect that the predominant method of lethal injection would have been at least as thoroughly studied as electrocution was before being implemented by New York state in 1890. However, it seems that the most common method of executing by lethal injection was developed by Oklahoma's medical examiner after several physicians refused to participate in the project, citing the Hippocratic Oath. That medical examiner's three-drug process has become the standard for lethal injection, but when asked why he chose those three drugs, he responded, "Why not?"[14]

To describe any method as the standard may be a stretch, given that there are nearly no standards governing lethal injection in some of the states using it. Some require doctors to be present, while others do not; some have extensive written protocols, while others either do not have such thorough protocols or refuse to divulge any protocol they might have.[15] Some states, meanwhile, seem thoroughly uninterested in the proper administration of lethal injection. Alan Doerhoff, the surgeon in Missouri who mixed the lethal dosages for executions in that state, admitted in a deposition that he did not know of a written protocol, and he believed he had the ability to change it if he wanted anyway. Further, he conceded that he relied on his memory when mixing the drugs, and concluded that "it's not unusual for me to make mistakes. . . . But I am dyslexic and that is the reason why there are inconsistencies in my testimony."[16] Doerhoff was finally relieved from his duties after the press reported that he had been sued for malpractice more than twenty times.[17]

Although there are other variations, about twenty-seven of the thirty-six states using lethal injection rely on a similar formula, comprised of three parts and following the example of Oklahoma.[18]

That process isn't complex, and it utilizes fairly common substances. First, an anesthetic is used. Typically, a surgical anesthetic called sodium thiopental, a short-acting barbiturate, is given to induce a deep sleep and sometimes a loss of consciousness, so that the condemned person will feel less pain as the other drugs are administered.[19]

The second step immobilizes the body. This second drug, often pancuronium bromide (which has the brand name Pavulon), has the effect of paralyzing the prisoner so that there is no struggle, screaming, or convulsing as the killing drug is administered in the third step. Notably, Pavulon does not affect the awareness of the person receiving it; it does not make the prisoner unconscious. Rather, it binds the muscles and masks the effects of the third drug for the comfort of the observers and the ease of the executioner.[20]

Finally, the third drug is meant to kill the condemned person. Most often, this is potassium chloride, which stops the heart in what is normally a very painful process—basically, a cardiac arrest.[21]

One danger of this process is that there is no way to evaluate whether the sedative, administered in the first step, is working. Once the second drug immobilizes the prisoner, observers cannot tell if he is dying peacefully in his sleep or he is fully conscious while his heart convulses; he will look the same either way. In recent litigation in California, both sides agreed that the last two drugs (the paralyzing and killing agents), administered to a conscious person, would cause an unconstitutional amount of pain. The court in that case also found that nearly half of the executions reviewed reflected that "inmates' breathing may not have ceased as expected."[22]

While it is not clear how this three-step process has persisted as long as it has, it is clear that it is problematic in a way that should be obvious. Nineteen states including Texas, the capital punishment capital of the United States, have actually outlawed the use of the combination of a paralyzing agent (Pavulon) in conjunction with a sedative (like sodium thiopental), because of the risk of the paralyzing agent masking the suffering of the subject. This restriction, however, applies only to animals that are being killed through euthanasia, not to human beings on death row.[23] Thus, while this procedure is not fit for a dog, it is the only method of execution allowable in many jurisdictions.

There is a second danger as well. A recent medical report concluded that if the sedative and the third drug, potassium chloride, fail to kill the prisoner, he may well die of the effects of the large dose of Pavulon, the paralyzing agent. If this is true, then the actual cause of death in at least some executions might be asphyxiation— the same thing that might have been the true cause of Christ's death on the cross.[24]

One fascinating aspect of the juxtaposition of Christ's experience and the process of lethal injection used in most states is that we have somehow chosen a method of execution that seeks to replicate through chemical means the steps of the Roman crucifixion to which Christ was subjected—anesthesia, disabling, and death. The fact that Christ refused the anesthesia should not change this analysis; rather, it may in some minds put Jesus in the place of the prisoner who is not administered a proper amount of sedative and feels the pain of either asphyxiation or the destruction of the heart.

Another odd fact about all this is that it isn't really necessary to use three drugs. If we chose, we could simply administer a sufficiently high dosage of the sedative, a barbiturate, which would both sedate the prisoner and kill him.[25]

There is no question that the cross was a far more inhumane form of execution than even the most botched lethal injection. Death by crucifixion was chosen expressly to inflict pain, while lethal injection at least does not have that as a goal. No one would argue that lethal injection comes close to causing the pain, at least for a duration, that crucifixion did. At most, in following the same basic steps, lethal injection faintly traces the effects of being hung on a cross.

Still, shouldn't it trouble us that our method of execution faintly traces the manner in which Christ was killed, in kind if not degree? The underlying wrong behind crucifixion was its outright and intentional cruelty. The underlying wrong with lethal injection is a hidden cruelty, the masked pain and unheard scream that the chemical combination, on dog or human, can create. While this is not the same as the cross, is allowing this procedure good enough for the standards that our God might demand of us as we deal with the least of those among us?

FORFEITURE

When the soldiers had crucified Jesus, they took his clothes and divided them into four parts, one for each soldier. They also took his tunic; now the tunic was seamless, woven in one piece from the top. So they said to one another, "Let us not tear it, but cast lots for it to see who will get it."   —John 19:23-24

E ach of the four Gospels tells us that the soldiers who were at the crucifixion divided up Jesus' clothes as he was dying on the cross (Matt 27:35; Mark 15:24; Luke 23:34; John 19:23-24). This grisly detail not only adds to the pathos of the scene but also foreshadows yet another sometimes troubling aspect of modern criminal law: the taking of a criminal's possessions, often for the benefit of the arresting agencies, in a process given the innocuous-sounding name of forfeiture. Because law enforcement agencies often get most of the money raised through forfeitures, part of the danger created is that the quest for funding will skew the motivations of the investigators to go after the cases that will offer the biggest payoff rather than those that will make the biggest difference.

The Gospels' descriptions of the dividing of Jesus' clothes were not meaningless observations, even taking aside any legal implications. Rather, the division of clothes continues the linkage of Jesus' death with the prophecies of Psalm 22 in the Old Testament, which begins with a foretelling of Jesus' cry from the cross: "My God, my God, why have you forsaken me?" (v. 1). Specifically, that psalm (written hundreds of years before Jesus' birth) forecast the conditions of the crucifixion:

> For dogs are all around me;
>   a company of evildoers encircles me.
> My hands and feet have shriveled;
> I can count all my bones.
> They stare and gloat over me;
> they divide my clothes among themselves,
>   and for my clothing they cast lots. (Ps 22:16-18)

The normal Roman practice was to crucify prisoners naked,[1] so the division of Jesus' clothes would be a plausible part of the scene. The casting of lots for the clothes is an interesting twist; commentators have guessed that the soldiers either threw dice to decide or played the still popular game of guessing how many fingers someone is holding up behind his back.[2]

According to John, the soldiers put Jesus' clothes into four piles, then were left with his tunic, which was a long garment worn next to the skin (John 19:23-24). The fact that the tunic was seamless created a quandary since it could not be divided up. To do so would destroy it. Most experts (though not all) have felt that the seamless tunic was a special thing: either a highly unusual garment, such as that worn by royalty, or more simply a normal garment of particularly good quality.[3]

Other things could have been done with Jesus' clothes, of course. They could have been given to his followers, who were present; left on him to retain some dignity as he died; or simply abandoned. That the guards took them, however, brings us to the more modern debate over forfeiture.

Forfeiture is the process by which the government takes ownership of property that may have a connection to crime. In the United States today the forfeiture of property and cash to the government has, in some areas, become a major source of funding for law enforcement. Some claim that the desire to forfeit cars, homes, and boats has driven the police to seek forfeiture even where patent unfairness would result.

One well-publicized forfeiture case, *Bennis v. Michigan*,[4] made it to the United States Supreme Court and brought to public attention the types of things that were being forfeited. Tina Bennis lost her car to forfeiture when her husband drove it out to pick up a prostitute and have sex. After her husband was arrested, the state declared the car a public nuisance and took it. As one would expect, Tina Bennis complained that she did not even know what her husband was doing with the car, and that she should not lose her Pontiac because of his illegal acts. The United States Supreme Court ruled against her, holding that Michigan's process violated neither the due process clause nor the takings clause of the Constitution.[5]

Cases like *Bennis* did not sit well with some voters. In 2001, Oregon voters passed a ballot measure that limited the ability of law enforcement agencies in that state to pursue certain kinds of forfeitures, and part of the impetus for that reform was the belief that the seizure of property was becoming a principal goal of law enforcement. After the measure passed, one supporter said, "Measure 3 passed because forfeiture was one of the largest funding sources for the specialty law enforcement teams around the state. They therefore had an incentive to take property that was profitable while overlooking other criminal activities with less 'profit' built in."[6]

On the other hand, many people in and out of government defend the use of forfeitures even with the risks they present. Proponents of broad forfeiture rules argue that forfeitures have the appealing result of simultaneously preventing crime and funding law enforcement.[7] In my experience as a federal prosecutor, I used forfeitures in conjunction with indictments to shut down illegal businesses, including a large-scale fencing ring. The advantage of this device is that it quickly puts a criminal enterprise out of business by depriving it of the means to make money. If you take the place of business, the customers don't know where to go; if you take the criminals' money, they lose the capital they need to ply their trade.

Generally, two categories of property can be seized and then forfeited: first, property (such as a house or a car) that was used to conduct the crime, and second, property that was purchased with proceeds from a crime. So, if you deliver cocaine to Chicago in your car, your car can be forfeited; if you sell a batch of cocaine in Chicago and buy a hot new car with the money you make, that car can be forfeited too.

Procedurally, there are no less than three distinct types of forfeitures. The easiest (from the standpoint of the government anyway) is usually called *administrative forfeiture*, which involves unclaimed property. The second easiest is *civil forfeiture*, in which a civil case is filed claiming ownership of the property for the government. The most difficult type of forfeiture for the government is *criminal forfeiture*, in which the claim over property is included in a criminal indictment and heard as part of the criminal trial.

Administrative forfeiture usually involves the government converting over to its ownership property that it already has in its possession. For example, if a bank robber is caught in the act and his car is left in the parking lot, while he is in jail or prison the car will be towed to an impound lot. If it is not claimed within a set period of time (say, thirty days), the government will take possession of the car and sell it at auction. Administrative forfeiture is easy for the government because no court case need be filed.

There is, of course, an underlying problem with administrative forfeiture in conjunction with a criminal case, at least from the perspective of the person whose property is being forfeited—being in jail or prison may make it hard to claim the car or other property. One may not be able to make arrangements to pick up property like a car, and mail service in some jails is not very good. In 2002, the United States Supreme Court heard a case involving this issue. The petitioner was a federal prisoner who was locked up at the prison in Milan, Michigan. While he was in confinement, the FBI filed for the administrative forfeiture of more than twenty thousand dollars in cash that it had seized from his home during a search, which led to his conviction. When the FBI got no response from the prisoner within the twenty days allowed, the agency took the money and gave it to the U.S. Marshal Service. The prisoner tried to get the money back once he became aware of the seizure, but the Supreme Court upheld the transfer of the money into the government's pocket, saying that it was adequate for the FBI to send notices by certified mail to three addresses, including the prison in Milan.[8]

Civil forfeiture is perhaps the most controversial. Unlike administrative forfeitures, civil forfeitures involve the filing of a court case. However, this case is a civil action that allows for a lessened burden of proof (more probable than not, rather than beyond a reasonable doubt) and the possibility of summary judgment for the government. Unlike criminal forfeitures, civil forfeitures do not require the conviction of the defendant first. Historically, the advantages to civil forfeitures have created a problematic temptation to law enforcement officials and prosecutors—to pursue civil forfeiture rather than to try for a criminal conviction.[9] This temptation is easy to understand if the criminal enterprise can be shut down simply through the forfeitures, and a principal goal of the prosecution is thus achieved without even filing a criminal case.

The abuses that result from the strange incentives of civil forfeiture connected to criminal cases have led to a few substantial reforms. The ballot initiative passed in Oregon, for example, virtually halted what had been a steady stream of civil forfeitures.[10] At the federal level, Congress passed the Civil Asset Forfeiture Reform Act of 2000, which limited the ability of the government to seize property through a civil action without meeting a tougher set of standards. As one commentator put it, these limits were put in place "partly in the recognition that law enforcement agencies have a financial stake in forfeiture, which creates the risk of overly aggressive enforcement."[11] Although Oregon and the federal government have put some limits on the worst abuses of forfeiture, other jurisdictions have not.

At the crucifixion, the soldiers divided the loot among themselves, and this aspect continues to mark forfeitures of property. Forfeitures that come through the federal program, for example, send about 80 percent of the value of forfeitures back to the participating law enforcement agencies, creating high incentives to participate in such programs and rewarding those with federal and state agencies with the most power or involvement in cases that generate forfeitures, such as large-scale narcotics investigations. For example, in Nebraska, the state patrol grabs most of the federal money given out from forfeitures, leaving little for the local law enforcement agencies.[12] In Missouri, the state constitution requires that forfeitures in drug cases benefit public schools, but for a while the police carrying out narcotics arrests made an end run around that requirement by turning the forfeitures over to the federal government, which then gave the proceeds back to them for their own uses.[13]

Forfeiture is distinct from the division of Jesus' clothes, of course. While the property of convicts continues to be split up among those involved, perhaps it is significant that the property at issue is different. Instead of a tunic and a small pile of clothes, now we are dividing up the money from cars and boats and homes.

Or perhaps not so different. Raymond Brown notes that nakedness was an especially bad deprivation of dignity to Jesus' people—as he puts it, there was a "Jewish horror of nudity."[14] Thus, the forfeiture of his clothes specifically had the effect of depriving Jesus of status in his society. If there is a corresponding "horror" in our society, it might be the fear of poverty, especially among those who are willing to commit criminal acts in order to accumulate wealth. Could it be that in our society, which worships wealth, taking away the markers of status—the cars, the boats, the homes—is in part desirable because it achieves the same effect as stripping Jesus of his clothes would have had? As the soldiers punished Jesus by taking and dividing his clothes, perhaps we do the same thing (with a much better aim, of course) by stripping criminals of their things in order to take away their status in society.

I have no trouble with that. A drug dealer should not return to society with the things he used to impress those around him. I have no sympathy if he walks out of prison and no longer has a nice car or a boat. As advocates of forfeiture say, these conversions achieve multiple goals, and perhaps one is the taking of status through wealth (or at least its trappings).

But what of Tina Bennis, whose husband used her car to visit a prostitute? Perhaps, as the little she had was taken, *she* is more like Christ than we are comfortable with.

CHAPTER SEVENTEEN

THE PROBLEM OF INNOCENCE

It was now about noon, and darkness came over the whole land until three in the afternoon, while the sun's light failed; and the curtain of the temple was torn in two. Then Jesus, crying with a loud voice, said, "Father, into your hands I commend my spirit." Having said this, he breathed his last. When the centurion saw what had taken place, he praised God and said, "Certainly this man was innocent."   —*Luke 23:44-47*

O f the many arguments against the death penalty, perhaps the one that is most compelling is this: the widespread use of the death penalty within an imperfect legal system inevitably leads to state executions of citizens who are, in fact, innocent.

The killing of an innocent is an affront to the conscience of almost all of us. We see this element of common conscience manifested in other areas of our public discourse: in the cries against legal abortion, for example, or the outcry against the killing of civilians in times of war. Outrage over the killing of an innocent man or woman is a core reason that we have the death penalty in the first place. Murder that is not justified as self-defense is so universally condemned that we as a state or nation feel the need to call for the ultimate punishment to exact retribution. Our many societies have few core values in common, but a condemnation of killing of innocents seems to be one of them.

This core value of not killing innocents has motivated one of the most dramatic political actions of modern times. In 2003, Governor George Ryan of Illinois emptied Illinois's death row. Over the course of two days, he pardoned 4 prisoners and commuted the death sentences of 167 others. As Amherst College professor Austin Sarat describes in his wonderful book *Mercy on Trial*, Ryan had been an outspoken supporter of the death penalty, and few people expected this change of heart at the time of the conservative governor's election:

> This white-haired, sixty-nine-year-old former pharmacist from Kankakee, Illinois, did not fit anyone's stereotype of either demon or hero, much less of the kind of national and international celebrity his clemency decision would make him. Nothing in his personality, or prior political record, suggested he would make much of a splash during his gubernatorial term or become a key national anti-death penalty activist. Ryan himself noted, "I mean, I am a Republican pharmacist from Kankakee. All of a sudden I've got gays and lesbians on my side. African-Americans. Senators from Italy, groups from around the world. It's a little surprising."[1]

What accounted for this radical transformation in a man who in 1977 was such a supporter of capital punishment that he had responded in the affirmative to a fellow legislator's challenge that those who supported the death penalty should have to throw the switch?

Sarat suggests that one strong factor in Ryan's dramatic shift was the unraveling of several cases pertaining to prisoners scheduled for execution. The first of them involved Anthony Porter, a man with an IQ of 51 who had been convicted in a double homicide. His conviction and sentence had been upheld by the state and federal courts, and he was scheduled for execution in 1998. However, two days before that execution a judge granted a stay based on the issue of mental disability. While the stay was in effect, a Northwestern University journalism professor and his students researched the case. They ultimately obtained a videotaped confession from another man who had actually committed the murders.[2]

After the Porter case and a series of articles in the *Chicago Tribune* revealed racial bias and strong patterns of incompetence in capital cases, Ryan chose to impose a moratorium on executions in 2000, three years before his broad grant of clemency. At the time of the moratorium, he also formed a Governor's Commission on Capital Punishment that was charged with reviewing the death penalty system in Illinois and recommending changes so that "no innocent person would ever again be sentenced to death in Illinois."[3]

After that commission's report was received and the revelation of the problems relating to innocence was made public, Ryan decided to issue the broad commutations. Some questioned his motivations, given that he was under investigation by federal prosecutors, who eventually convicted him on corruption charges. Victims' rights groups were also upset at the decision, and the sister of one victim said of such murder victims that Ryan's decision "killed them all over again."[4]

While the commutations received most of the press attention, perhaps it is the four pardons that are more remarkable—those four men went from sitting on death row, waiting to be killed, to walking out of prison for the simple reason that they were innocent. The day after the pardons and commutations were completed, Governor Ryan gave a speech at the Northwestern University School of Law. In that speech, he spoke movingly of the findings of innocence and the role they played in undermining his belief in the death penalty:

> As I reported yesterday, there is not a doubt in my mind that the number of innocent men freed from our Death Row stands at 17, with the pardons of Aaron Patterson, Madison Hobley, Stanley Howard and Leroy Orange.
>
> This is an absolute embarrassment. 17 exonerated death row inmates is nothing short of a catastrophic failure. But the 13, now 17 men, is just the beginning of our sad arithmetic in prosecuting murder cases. During the time we have had capital punishment in Illinois, there were at least 33 other people wrongly convicted on murder charges and exonerated. Since we reinstated the death penalty there are also 93 people—93—where our criminal justice system imposed the most severe sanction and later rescinded the sentence or even released them from custody because they were innocent.

How many more cases of wrongful conviction have to occur before we can all agree that the system is broken?[5]

The crisis in Illinois did not occur in isolation. The advent of DNA evidence has led to a cascade of innocence claims by death row inmates, many of them legitimate. In the preface to their book *Actual Innocence*, Jim Dwyer, Peter Neufeld, and Barry Scheck describe a scene that reflects the extent of innocence questions in the wake of DNA testing and other scientific advances. One of their clients, Dennis Fritz, was about to be released from prison on a murder charge, having proved his innocence. As his case for release developed, a television network followed the progress closely, hoping to do a story on Fritz once he was released. By the time that day came, however, the network was no longer interested. "I'm really sorry," a network executive explained, "but my bosses think there are too many of these stories going around. He's just another one of these innocent guys getting out."[6]

The scope of these "innocent guys getting out" was perhaps best described in an article produced by a group of scholars at the University of Michigan with the dry title of "Exonerations in the United States 1989–2003."[7] While acknowledging that they were able to identify only some of the exonerations during that period and that they did not include mass exonerations (such as those resulting from the scandal in Tulia, Texas), they described 340 exonerations of convicted defendants in major cases. Of that 340, 60 percent had been convicted for murder, and nearly all the rest were convicted of sexual assault or rape. Of those 205 exonerations in murder cases, 74 involved death row inmates who, like Anthony Porter, went from death row to freedom (in the absence of other charges).

The findings of the University of Michigan team are startling for what they show about convictions of those about to be executed and about those who already had been executed. Relating to those already dead, the authors noted a troubling calculation:

> Finally, the frequency of exonerations from death row is a chilling reminder of the consequences of these false convictions. If we managed to identify and release 75% of innocent death-row

inmates before they were put to death, then we also executed twenty-five innocent defendants from 1989 through 2003. If, somehow, we have caught 90% of false capital convictions, then we only executed eight innocent defendants in that fifteen-year period. Is it conceivable that a system that produces all these horrendous errors in the first place could also detect and correct 90% of those errors, after the fact? And considering the number of mistakes in capital trials, even an unlikely 90% exoneration rate would be disturbingly low.[8]

It seems that the question is not whether or not we are executing innocents, but how many we are executing.

In such an atmosphere, perhaps what is shocking is not that Governor Ryan of Illinois examined and upended the system, but that he is, to date, almost alone in wanting to even know if the system is broken. Other governors in states with the death penalty have chosen instead not to examine the system, preferring to assume that the machinery works perfectly and provides no chance for the execution of innocents. For example, Governor Jeb Bush of Florida is a proponent of the death penalty and a pro-life opponent of legal abortion. Asked to justify his lack of a consistent pro-life position, he simply explained that "taking an innocent life is wrong."[9]

Inherent in Bush's philosophy is the assumption that capital punishment never takes innocent life, even as the facts about the Illinois cases were coming to light. Tellingly, Bush never bothered to find out if there were similar problems in his state by commissioning an intensive study such as the one that brought forth such troubling facts in Illinois.

As Governor Bush declined to follow Governor Ryan's lead, so did other governors across the country. Sadly, the library shelves are not stocked with state examinations of whether they are executing innocents. Rather, they are filled with studies such as the 1986 Meese Commission Report on Pornography, compiled after months of meetings and study, totaling nearly three thousand pages in two bound volumes and leading to little besides exposing the silly fact that there is, somewhere in America, a pornographic/patriotic novel titled *Of Thee I Swing*.[10] Probably it should not be surprising that U.S. Attorney General Edwin Meese did not worry about innocence on death row as much as he did about pornography. Like Jeb Bush, he assumed that the system of criminal law was perfect, saying, "The thing is, you don't have many suspects who are innocent of a crime. That's contradictory. If a person is innocent of a crime, then he is not a suspect."[11]

Given the importance of innocence questions in the debate over the death penalty, what does Christianity have to add to the discussion?

Perhaps most important, it offers a reason to care about innocence, given that the tragic and glorious story at the center of the faith is about the execution of an innocent—tragic in its condemnation of human beings and our rush to judgment, and glorious in its portrayal of the power and grace of God.

The Bible takes pains to point out the innocence of Christ in the specific context of his trial, conviction, appeals, and execution. Specifically, two actors in the trial and execution seemed stricken with guilt at their actions due to Christ's innocence, including one of the Roman centurions standing guard at Golgotha and Pontius Pilate.

At the time of the execution, the Gospels described the conversion of one of the executioners, a Roman centurion, who recognized this crucial fact (Matt 27:54; Mark 15:39; Luke 23:47). It appears that this centurion was assigned the task of watching over the proceedings, and he would have seen the full drama. He was there representing the empire, the very empire that had sanctioned the killing through its representative, Pilate. After Jesus died (which coincided with darkness falling over the land), the centurion was moved by what he saw and cried out, "Certainly this man was innocent" (Luke 23:47). This centurion (like Governor Ryan) was unique among his peers. Other centurions were present at various stages, but filled their predictable roles as government functionaries in mocking the condemned man, leading him away to the execution place, crucifying him, and dividing his possessions (Mark 15:16-24). The importance of innocence was not equally clear to all present.

Pilate, in a more consistent and at times subtle way, also declared that Jesus might have been innocent. When the chief priests brought Jesus to Pilate after his conviction, his response after questioning the convict was, "I find no basis for an accusation against this man" (Luke 23:4). Nevertheless, as discussed previously, Pilate yielded to political pressure at the time of the appeal and sent Christ on to Herod.

That was not Pilate's last statement regarding Christ's innocence, either. At the time of the crucifixion, a sign was placed over Jesus' cross proclaiming, "Jesus of Nazareth, the King of the Jews" (John 19:19). The chief priests urged Pilate to change the sign to read, "This man said, I am King of the Jews" (John 19:21), but Pilate refused, saying, "What I have written I have written" (John 19:22).

Intriguingly, this recognition of Jesus' innocence may be in part the basis for the respect that Pilate is accorded in some Christian circles—surprising given that he was such a central figure in the legal proceedings and execution of Christ. There is a gnostic gospel, *The Gospel of Pilate*, that (predictably) is highly sympathetic to the prelate. Some thought that Pilate died in what is now Vienna, and Mount Pilate outside that city is named for him, as is the larger Mount Pilatus near Lucerne. The Greek Orthodox Church has even set aside a day, October 27, to honor Pilate's wife, Procla.[12]

To the Christian, one does not need the word of Pontius Pilate or an unnamed Roman centurion to believe that Christ was innocent. The raw fact that Christians believe Jesus was, in fact, the Son of God disproves to us the charge of blasphemy. It is a simple and basic article of the faith that Jesus died for our sins, not because of his own, as the chief priests urged.

How could a Christian hold apart the issue of innocence in our modern law from the tragic and wonderful fact of innocence that is at the center of our faith? That the Savior of humanity suffered such an injustice must mean something, must have some import.

I have heard many academics argue that innocence should not be such a prominent part of the debate over the death penalty. For example, David Dow, a campaigner against the death penalty and the author of *Executed on a Technicality: Lethal Injustice on America's Death Row*,[13] has argued in a *New York Times* column that the issue of innocence detracts from a close examination of the flawed procedures in the trials of innocent and guilty persons. In that column, he concludes that "innocence is a distraction."[14]

As a Christian, I disagree; the fact that some people (perhaps not many, but some) may even today share the fate of Christ resounds within me in a way it would not in those who do not share my ideas about Christ. In other words, the Gospels not only contain a series of lessons; they also tell Christians what issues are important. Through each of his actions, Christ was a teacher, and this must be especially true in the giving of his life. If we choose to worship an innocent who was executed as a criminal, shouldn't we care about the execution of innocents in our time? Can we in good conscience continue to abide by a system that will continue to execute a large number of the guilty and a smaller number of the innocent, given a faith that values each life so dearly?

Perhaps it says something of our collective conscience that politicians so often react to the problem of innocence by pretending that it is an impossibility under our legal system. It is easier for them to cling to this calming, ridiculous fiction than to deal with the more apparent truth and justify to the public the fact that from time to time the state will sweep up an innocent man in the dead of night, charge him with a crime he did not commit, parade him before a judge at arraignment, make his charges public, humiliate him and his family, pursue his execution through appeal and habeas, feed him a celebrated last meal, and then put him to a painful death while repeating with great moral indignation the false accusations against him.

It seems that it would be difficult for an intelligent, engaged politician, be it Bill Clinton or George Bush, to justify his support for a death penalty that kills innocents if he returns home on the weekend, goes to church with his family, hears from the Bible that "truly I tell you, just as you did not do it to one of the least of these, you did not do it to me" (Matt 25:45), and looks up to see a statue of a man on a cross.

Or perhaps, given the history of Christian support for such a death penalty, it is not as hard as I imagine.

CHAPTER EIGHTEEN

ALONENESS AND THE ETHICS OF THE CROWD

"But all of this has taken place, so that the scriptures of the prophets may be fulfilled." Then all the disciples deserted him and fled.
—Matthew 26:56

The disciples deserted him, and Jesus died alone and without supporters in front of a crowd gathered to cheer on the spectacle (Luke 23:48). Even his acquaintances "stood at a distance" so as to avoid detection (Luke 23:49). The sense of aloneness, the actions of a mob—among the many familiars in the Gospel, these are among the most compelling.

Recently I was alone in West Texas, a place where it is still possible to be very, very alone—possible, even, to stop square in the middle of a straight, flat road, get out, and see a million stars as you stand on the roof of your car. I was driving west through the hulking Davis Mountains, heading toward the high desert town of Marfa.

Among the many eccentric towns in Texas, Marfa is especially intriguing. It is known for the Marfa lights, balls of fire that travel through the desert near town with no apparent explanation. However, the paranormal phenomena around Marfa are probably less interesting than the human interactions in and around the place. In 1971, a minimalist artist from New York named Donald

Judd came to town and eventually acquired two airplane hangars and a decommissioned military base to house enormous art installations. The population of about three thousand now consists of a strange mix of artists and ranchers, and the town contains an unusual number of art galleries, fancy restaurants, and performance spaces for a tiny community in the middle of West Texas. The ground and the sky remain unchanged, though, looking just as they were depicted in the 1956 James Dean and Elizabeth Taylor movie *Giant*, which made great use of those huge, unbroken spaces.

Driving westward on highway 67, I followed the road that wound through the mountains and then down into the flat, barren desert. By the time I got to Marfa, I was glad to see people and cross streets and a gas station. I got out of the car, not knowing what I would find. I walked down the dusty main street and saw a long, flat pane of glass that I soon realized was a heavy, extravagant door. It swung easily once I shifted my weight into it, and as it gave way, I felt that familiar blast of air-conditioning.

There was no one in the immense room. It was a spare and stark space, with a beautiful and expensive wood floor, devoid of furniture save an elegant desk and chair positioned near the wall of glass. The room was not empty, though, even without people and furniture. It was an art gallery.

Before me, on the wall, was an enormous and striking painting. Jesus sat at a long table, surrounded by men arguing with one another, gesturing and imploring. I had seen representations of the Last Supper before, but never like this. The familiar characters at the table were washed over with strips of green, red, and yellow, and the very size of the painting was overwhelming.

Silently, a door opened at the far end of the hall, and a well-tailored woman walked in.

"What is this?" I asked.

"It's the Last Supper," she explained patiently. "The last meal Jesus had before he died."

The artist, I found, was Andy Warhol. *Last Supper* was one of more than one hundred images of that event he produced, creating most of them by hand-drawing and silk-screening the images from source material that included cheap reproductions of Leonardo da Vinci's famous painting of the event. It turns out that Warhol was a secretive but active Catholic, who attended Mass several times a week, prayed daily with his mother, helped feed the homeless persons at his church, and even had a private audience with the Pope in 1980.[1]

The woman, having explained, slipped back through the door, leaving me alone again with the huge images of Christ and his followers. It was a still, small moment.

I drove back to the east, the other way through the desert, as dusk fell. The rough earth and the scrubby brush might have been similar to what surrounded the path to Golgotha that Jesus walked with his cross. The terrain brought to mind a case I have taught, *Tison v. Arizona*, which was about death, retribution, and the desert. I like the case because of its subtlety and depth, though these are not easy for students to discern. One of my students once told me that I teach cases in a form that amounts to something like the hobbit game of "what's in my pocket?" and he was right. The life of a case is very often not in the conclusion and holding, but in the footnotes, the dissent, the choice of a word deep in an analysis, tucked into those places where the law allows bits of humanity to be hidden.

Tison was, on its face, a significant but not a landmark decision by the United States Supreme Court. The story, though, is compelling. Gary Tison was truly a dangerous man. He went to prison, then escaped by killing a guard. He was given a life sentence for this killing, and was returned to prison. His life of crime was not finished, though. He and his cell mate, Randy Greenawalt (also a convicted murderer), made plans to escape the prison again.[2]

Their plan worked. Tison's family members entered the prison carrying a large ice chest filled with guns. They quickly armed Tison and Greenawalt, locked the prison guards and visitors into a storage closet, and fled the grounds in a Ford Galaxy. Quickly and cleverly, they abandoned the Ford and picked up a Lincoln that they had previously hidden. They drove it to an isolated house.[3]

After two nights at the house, the group headed out through the high desert toward Flagstaff. They traveled back roads to avoid detection and were far from the beaten path when they suffered a blown tire that disabled the Lincoln. Needing a new car, they flagged down a passing Mazda, which was carrying four people: John Lyons, his wife, Donnelda, their two-year-old son, Christopher, and Lyons's fifteen-year-old niece, Theresa. The convicts forced the four into the Lincoln, which they then drove far into the desert. There, Gary Tison disabled the car by firing a shotgun into the radiator and told the four captives to line up in front of the car. While the victims begged for their lives, Gary Tison and Randy Greenawalt shot them, then left them in the desert, as the murderers escaped with their accomplices in the Mazda. Of the four victims, Theresa was the only one to survive, albeit briefly. She crawled away from the scene before dying alone in the desert.[4]

Gary Tison embodies perhaps the best argument in favor of the death penalty, in that he was given a life sentence for killing and then killed again in a particularly cruel and unnecessary way. As one might imagine, the public in Arizona was outraged by the crime. Gary Tison would not escape execution again. The problem, though, was that Gary Tison was no longer around to execute. He had died of exposure in the desert sun after the escape attempt fell apart days later.[5] Instead, a jury convicted and sentenced to death Ricky and Raymond Tison, Gary Tison's two sons, and their death sentences were upheld by the Supreme Court. At the time of the killings, Ricky and Raymond Tison were walking away from the scene to get water for the captives, not knowing that their father would kill the four as they stood in front of the Lincoln.[6]

The *Tison* case contains one of the most subtle and damning condemnations of one justice by another in the history of the Court. At that time the Supreme Court was split on death penalty cases. Four justices (Rehnquist, White, Powell, and Scalia) generally favored employing the death penalty, while four others (Brennan, Blackmun, Marshall, and Stevens) generally voted to restrict or eliminate the death penalty. In the middle as the swing vote was Justice Sandra Day O'Connor, who was from Arizona. In this case, as with many others, O'Connor's swing vote carried the day in favor of execution, and she also wrote the opinion for that 5–4 majority. The subtle condemnation came in the dissent by Justice William Brennan, who wrote:

> The murders that Gary Tison and Randy Greenawalt committed revolt and grieve all who learn of them. When the deaths of the Lyons family and Theresa Tyson were first reported, many in Arizona erupted into a "towering yell" for retribution and justice.[7]

Brennan then compared the case to 1923's *Moore v. Dempsey*,[8] in which the Supreme Court held that the defendants "were hurried to conviction under the pressure of a mob without any regard for their rights and without according them due process of the law."[9] Finally, having tied together the towering yell for retribution and the specter of a mob, Brennan quoted the book of Exodus, Horace, and finally Shakespeare's *Merchant of Venice* for the words "Yes, truly, for look you, the sins of the father are to be laid upon the children."[10] In whole, the message is clear: O'Connor the Arizonan is a part of the mob that has focused its anger on the children now that the father is gone.

The accusation is strikingly specific—that O'Connor did not come to her decision through her own deliberations, but through reaction to the crowd. And how ancient is that crowd, crying out, "Crucify him!"? At each moment of Christ's persecution, the crowd was there, pressing for death. To those making decisions, a moment of individual contemplation was not allowed, even to Herod or Pilate, both of whom were harangued by those seeking retribution as the officials deliberated the case.

Those instincts are strong in us—to join our voices in the condemnation, to be a part of the "towering yell." It brings us camaraderie, a sense of purpose, and the feeling of inclusion, and it is much safer than being the one to yell, "Stop!" But for those of us who are Christians, to which way of thinking are we called? Are we to be a part of that mob calling for retribution?

Not if we are to follow the example of Christ. In John 8, the Pharisees called Christ to the scene of an execution. There was no doubt that the defendant, an adulteress, was guilty; she was caught in the act. Nor was there doubt that the law called for execution for that offense. Jesus' response is oft-quoted:

> Jesus bent down and wrote with his finger on the ground. When they kept on questioning him, he straightened up and said to them, "Let anyone among you who is without sin be the first to throw a stone at her." And once again he bent down and wrote on the ground. (John 8:6-8)

The words of Jesus have deep meaning. It should affect a Christian's view of the death penalty that Christ came upon a legal execution and stopped it, saying that the executioners lacked the moral authority to exact that punishment. But there is something more to this story, something about how we think about this issue.

Christ's words seem clear, but what to make of the drawing on the ground? The Gospel does not tell us what Jesus wrote. Perhaps what he wrote isn't important; it could be that it was the very act of writing in the sand that mattered. By taking that moment to write on the ground, Christ removed himself from the mob and contemplated the question. In the end, this might be the example that Christ offers as we consider capital punishment, suggesting that we remove ourselves from the mob and quietly hold up the question before our consciences and faith. For those of us who follow a religion whose central narrative is an execution and its aftermath, we owe at least that to our God.

Notes

Introduction

1. Albert Camus, "Reflections on the Guillotine," *Resistance, Rebellion, and Death* (New York: Alfred A. Knopf, 1960).

3. The Use of a Paid Informant

1. Alexandra Natapoff, "Bait & Snitch: The High Cost of Snitching for Law Enforcement," *Slate*, December 12, 2006.
2. Ibid.
3. *The Gospel of Judas*, ed. Rodolphe Kasser, Marvin Meyer, and Gregor Wurst (Washington, D.C.: National Geographic Society, 2006).
4. MSNBC, "Inspector General: FBI Ignores Informant Rules," September 12, 2005, http://msnbc.msn.com/id/9317523.
5. Ibid.
6. Daniel C. Richman, "Cooperating Defendants: The Costs and Benefits of Purchasing Information from Scoundrels," *Federal Sentencing Reporter* 8 (March/April 1996): 292.
7. Raymond E. Brown, *The Death of the Messiah*, 2 vols. (New York: Doubleday, 1994), 1:641.
8. Ibid., 1:242.
9. *The Gospel of Judas*, 43.
10. Ibid.
11. Ibid., 45.
12. Brown, *Death of the Messiah*, 2:1399–1400.
13. Ibid., 2:1401.

4. Strategic Arrest

1. *United States v. Rahman*, 189 F3d 88 (2d Cir. 1999).
2. Ibid., at 111.

3. Daniel Richman, "Prosecutors and Their Agents, Agents and Their Prosecutors," *Colorado Law Review* 103 (2003): 749, 767n74.

4. *United States v. Branch*, 91 F3d 699, 709–10 (5th Cir. 1999).

5. Ibid., at 710.

6. Raymond E. Brown, *The Death of the Messiah*, 2 vols. (New York: Doubleday, 1994), 1:247.

7. Ibid.

8. Ibid., 1:248.

9. Ibid., 1:249.

10. Alan Watson, *The Trial of Jesus* (Athens: University of Georgia Press, 1995), 48.

5. The Maiming of the Slave and the Role of Power

1. Luke 6:29 ("If anyone strikes you on the cheek, offer the other also; and from anyone who takes away your coat do not withhold even your shirt").

2. 18 U.S.C. §3592(b)(5).

3. Raymond E. Brown, *The Death of the Messiah*, 2 vols. (New York: Doubleday, 1994), 1:270.

4. Ibid.

5. Ibid., 1:271.

6. Robert Darden, *Reluctant Prophets and Clueless Disciples: Introducing the Bible by Telling Its Stories* (Nashville: Abingdon Press, 2006), 139–56.

7. According to Matthew, Jesus said, "But all this has taken place, so that the scriptures of the prophets may be fulfilled" (26:56).

8. W. W. Buckland, *The Roman Law of Slavery* (New York: AMS Press, 1969), 3–5.

9. Harold Remus, *Jesus as Healer* (New York: Cambridge University Press, 1997), 58. Remus recounts such acclamations at Luke 5:26; 7:16; 9:43; 13:13; and 18:43.

10. 408 U.S. 238 (1972).

11. Ibid., at 255–56.

12. Ibid., at 364, quoting 1968 hearings before the Subcommittee on Criminal Laws and Procedures of the Senate Committee on the Judiciary, 90th Cong., 2d sess.

13. Ibid., at 366.

14. *Gregg v. Georgia*, 428 U.S. 153 (1976).

15. 481 U.S. 279 (1987).

16. Mark Osler, "Indirect Harms and Proportionality: The Upside-Down World of Federal Sentencing," *University of Mississippi Law Journal* 74 (2005): 1.

17. United States Sentencing Commission, *Report to Congress: Cocaine and Federal Sentencing Policy*, May 2002, chapter 5, http://www.ussc.gov.

6. The Initial Appearance

1. Alan Watson, *The Trial of Jesus* (Athens: University of Georgia Press, 1995), 48.
2. Texas Code of Criminal Procedure, art. 2.09.
3. Raymond E. Brown, *The Death of the Messiah*, 2 vols. (New York: Doubleday, 1994), 1:405.
4. Simon Legasse, *The Trial of Jesus* (London: SCM Press, 1997), 44.
5. After Herod rejected the petition of Jesus, he returned to Pilate, but I would consider the modern analogy to this hearing to be a clemency hearing before execution, which would be before a governor and not a judge.
6. Robert Cochran, "How Do You Plead, Guilty or Not Guilty? Does the Plea Inquiry Violate the Defendant's Right to Silence?" *Cardozo Law Review* 26 (2005): 1409.
7. Ibid.
8. Ibid.
9. *United States v. Salerno*, 481 U.S. 739 (1987).

7. Last Meal / Last Supper

1. Allan Turner, "Last Meals Considered Tasteless," *Houston Chronicle*, December 15, 2003. This article reported on the discontinuation of the menu listings in 2003 after some citizens complained. The log is partially preserved, however, at http://www.thememoryhole.org/deaths/texas-final-meals.htm.
2. Brian Price, "The Last Supper," *Legal Affairs*, March/April 2004, http://www.legalaffairs.org/printerfriendly.msp?id=536.
3. Brian Price, *Meals to Die For* (London: Artnik, 2004), 452, 470, 477.
4. Ibid., 101–3.
5. Snoop Dogg, *Tha Last Meal* (Priority Records, 2000).
6. Turner, "Last Meals Considered Tasteless."
7. Jacquelyn C. Black, . . . *Last Meal* (Monroe, Maine: Common Courage Press, 2003), 18.
8. Ibid., 46.
9. Ibid., 26, 34, 37.

8. The Fact of a Trial

1. For example, Francois Bovon, *The Last Days of Jesus*, trans. Kristin Hennessy (Louisville: Westminster John Knox Press, 2006).
2. Raymond E. Brown, *The Death of the Messiah*, 2 vols. (New York: Doubleday, 1994), 1:476.
3. Ibid., 1:438.

4. Ibid., 2:1101.

5. For example, "Trial and Errors: The Detroit Terror Case; After Convictions, the Undoing of a U.S. Terror Prosecution," *New York Times*, 1A, October 7, 2004.

6. Brown, *Death of the Messiah*, 1:435.

7. Texas Code of Criminal Procedure, art. 38.13.

9. The Trial Witnesses

1. Frank O. Bowman, "Departing Is Such Sweet Sorrow: A Year of Judicial Revolt on 'Substantial Assistance' Departures Follows a Decade of Prosecutorial Indiscipline," *Stetson Law Review* 29 (1999): 7, 15.

2. Ellen Yaroshefsky, "Cooperation with Federal Prosecutors: Experiences of Truth Telling and Embellishment," *Fordham Law Review* 68 (1999): 917, 939.

3. Ibid., 954.

4. Ellen Yaroshefsky, "Wrongful Convictions: It Is Time to Take Prosecution Discipline Seriously," *University of the District of Columbia Law Review* 8 (2004): 275, 276.

5. 144 F3 1343 (10th Cir. 1998), reversed en banc 165 F3d 1297 (10th Cir. 1999), certiorari denied 527 U.S. 1024 (1999).

6. 165 F3d 1297 (10th Cir.), certiorari denied 527 U.S. 1024 (1999).

7. Yaroshefsky, "Cooperation with Federal Prosecutors," 917, 939.

8. This interpretation of Mark was first suggested to me by Dr. Mary Darden.

9. United States Sentencing Commission data, http://www.ussc.gov/jud pack/1998/pae98.pdf.

10. Nationally, federal rates of downward departures for cooperation remain well over 30 percent for such cases; see http://www.ussc.gov.

10. The Prosecutor's Emotion

1. Texas Code of Criminal Procedure, art. 2.01.

2. 477 U.S. 168 (1986).

3. Ibid., 180n12.

4. Ibid., 189n2 (Brennan, J. dissenting).

5. Ibid., 181.

6. Raymond E. Brown, *The Death of the Messiah*, 2 vols. (New York: Doubleday, 1994), 1:517.

7. Susan Bandes, "What's Love Got to Do with It?" *William and Mary Journal of Women and the Law* 8 (2001): 97, 100–101.

8. Ibid., 101.

9. Aristotle, *On Rhetoric*, trans. George A. Kennedy (New York: Oxford University Press, 1991), 8–10.

10. Ibid.

11. Ibid., 125.

12. Susan Bandes, "Loyalty to One's Convictions: The Prosecutor and Tunnel Vision," *Howard Law Journal* 49 (2006): 475, 476.

13. Ibid.

14. Ibid., 477.

15. Ibid.

16. Ibid., 486.

17. Ibid.

18. Ellen Yaroshefsky, "Cooperation with Federal Prosecutors: Experiences of Truth Telling and Embellishment," *Fordham Law Review* 68 (1999): 917, 949.

19. Brown, *Death of the Messiah*, 2:1426.

11. The Appeal to Pilate

1. The exception is the criminal prosecutor, who usually cannot appeal a jury verdict in the trial court because of the constitutional prohibition against double jeopardy.

2. Raymond E. Brown, *The Death of the Messiah*, 2 vols. (New York: Doubleday, 1994), 1:714n92.

3. Ibid.

4. Ibid.

5. Ibid.

6. Francoise Bovon, *The Last Days of Jesus*, trans. Kristin Hennessy (Louisville: Westminster John Knox Press, 2006) 37.

7. Jesus' response to this question is, "You say so," and the reporting of this exchange is one of the few times that all four Gospels agree precisely. See Brown, *Death of the Messiah*, 1:729.

8. *United States v. Looney*, slip opinion 06-10605 (5th Cir. June 23, 2008).

9. Ibid.

10. Michael Rowan, Comment, "Minding Our Skepticism: A Conservative Approach to Capital Punishment," *Florida State University Law Review* 31 (2004): 377, 398n139.

12. Habeas Denied

1. Eric M. Freedman, *Habeas Corpus: Rethinking the Great Writ of Liberty* (New York: New York University Press, 2001), 1.

2. Ronald P. Sokol, *Federal Habeas Corpus*, 2d ed. (Charlottesville, Va.: Michie Company, 1969), 3.

3. Raymond E. Brown, *The Death of the Messiah*, 2 vols. (New York: Doubleday, 1994), 1:763.

4. Ibid.

5. Ibid., 1:766.

6. Erik Degrate, "I'm Innocent: Can a California Innocence Project Help Exonerate Me? . . . Not if the Antiterrorism and Effective Death Penalty Act (AEDPA) Has Its Way," *Western State University Law Review* 34 (2006): 67, 78.

7. 28 U.S.C. §2244(d). This period is generally tolled while the prisoner is pursuing state habeas or in certain other, much rarer, circumstances.

8. 28 U.S.C. §2254(b)(1).

9. 28 U.S.C. §2254(d).

10. 28 U.S.C. §2244(d).

11. Florida Department of Corrections, Annual Report 2003–2004, M23, http://www.dc.state.fl.us/pub/annual/0304/pdfs/education.pdf.

12. Thomas C. O'Bryant, "The Great Unattainable Writ: Indigent Pro Se Litigation after the Antiterrorism and Effective Death Penalty Act of 1996," *Harvard Civil Rights—Civil Liberties Law Review* 41 (2006): 299, 307.

13. Ibid., 325.

14. Ibid., 323.

13. The Governor Denies Clemency

1. *Knote v. United States*, 95 U.S. 149, 153 (1877).

2. Texas Constitution, art. 4, sec. 11.

3. Vernon's Ann. Texas Constitution, art. 4, sec. 11, interpretive commentary (2007).

4. Victoria J. Palacios, "Faith in Fantasy: The Supreme Court's Reliance on Commutation to Ensure Justice in Death Penalty Cases," *Vanderbilt Law Review* 49 (1996): 311, 344.

5. Carol S. Steiker and Jordan M. Steiker, "A Tale of Two Nations: Implementation of the Death Penalty in 'Executing' versus 'Symbolism' States in the United States," *Texas Law Review* 84 (2006): 1869, 1906.

6. 506 U.S. 390 (1993).

7. The pathway to successfully making an innocence claim was clarified somewhat in *House v. Bell*, 126 S. Ct. 2064 (2006).

8. 506 U.S. at 411, quoted in Palacios, *"Faith in Fantasy,"* 311, 342–342.

9. Ibid., at 404.

10. *California v. Brown*, 479 U.S. 538 (1987).

11. *United States v. Wilson*, 32 U.S. 150, 160 (1833).

12. *Biddle v. Perovich*, 274 U.S. 480 (1927).

13. Palacios, "Faith in Fantasy," 311, 346.

14. Paul Whitlock Cobb Jr., "Reviving Mercy in the Structure of Capital Punishment," *Yale Law Journal* 99 (1989): 389, 394.

15. Palacios, "Faith in Fantasy," 350.

16. Ibid., 363.

17. Raymond E. Brown, *The Death of the Messiah*, 2 vols. (New York: Doubleday, 1994), 1:815.

18. Ibid.

19. Palacios, "Faith in Fantasy," 313.

14. Humiliation of the Convicted

1. Luke 22:63 seems to place this event between arrest and conviction.

2. Raymond E. Brown, *The Death of the Messiah*, 2 vols. (New York: Doubleday, 1994), 1:865–66.

3. John reported only that Jesus carried his own cross, while Mark described only that Simon was made to carry it. It is possible that both are true, of course.

4. Marcus J. Borg and John Dominic Crossan, *The Last Week: A Day-by-Day Account of Jesus's Final Week in Jerusalem* (San Francisco: HarperSanFrancisco, 2006).

5. Francois Bovon, *The Last Days of Jesus* (Louisville: Westminster John Knox Press 2006), 27.

6. Austin Sarat, "To See or Not to See: Why Timothy McVeigh's Execution Should Be Televised," http://writ.news.findlaw.com/commentary/20010405_sarat.html.

7. Stephan Groschwitz and Annulla Linders, "The Return of the Spectacle? The Modern Execution Event in the United States" (paper, American Sociological Association, Philadelphia, Penn., August 12, 2005), http://www.allacademic.com/meta/p21382_index.html.

8. Ryan J. Huschka, "Sorry for the Jackass Sentence: A Critical Analysis of the Constitutionality of Contemporary Shaming Punishments," *University of Kansas Law Review* 54 (2006): 803.

9. Ibid., 817.

10. *United States v. Gementera*, 379 F3d 596 (9th Cir. 2004).

11. Dan M. Kahan, "What Do Alternative Sanctions Mean?" *University of Chicago Law Review* 63 (1996): 591.

12. Dan M. Kahan, "What's Really Wrong with Shaming Sanctions," *Texas Law Review* 84 (2006): 2075.

13. *United States v. Gementera*, 379 F3d 596 (9th Cir. 2004).

14. Sharon Lamb, "The Psychology of Condemnation: Underlying Emotions and Their Symbolic Expression in Condemning and Shaming," *Brooklyn Law Review* 68 (2003): 929, 930.

15. Ibid., 942.

16. Ibid., 941.

15. A Cruel and Unusual Execution

1. Marcus J. Borg and John Dominic Crossan, *Last Week: A Day-by-Day Account of Jesus's Final Week in Jerusalem* (San Francisco: HarperSanFrancisco 2006), 146.

2. *Baze v. Rees*, 128 S. Ct. 1520, 1537 (2008).

3. Matthew said it was wine mixed with "gall" (27:34).

4. Raymond E. Brown, *The Death of the Messiah*, 2 vols. (New York: Doubleday, 1994), 2:941.

5. Ibid. Brown does not conclude, though, that the myrrh was necessarily used to ease the pain of crucifixion; it might have had some other purpose.

6. Brown describes a height of seven feet as "a common guess." Ibid., 2:949.

7. Ibid., 2:1090–91.

8. Ibid., 2:1091–92.

9. Deborah W. Denno, "The Lethal Injection Quandary: How Medicine Has Dismantled the Death Penalty," May 1, 2007, 7, http://ssrn.com/abstracts=983732.

10. Ibid., 8.

11. Ibid.

12. Ibid.

13. Note "A New Test for Evaluating Eighth Amendment Challenges to Lethal Injections," *Harvard Law Review* 120 (2007): 1301, 1302.

14. Ibid., 1309.

15. Deborah W. Denno, "When Legislatures Delegate Death: The Troubling Paradox Behind State Uses of Electrocution and Lethal Injection and What It Says about Us," *Ohio State Law Journal* 63 (2002): 147–80.

16. James R. Wong, "Lethal Injection Protocols: The Failure of Litigation to Stop Suffering and the Case for Legislative Reform," *Temple Journal of Science, Technology & Environmental Law* 25 (2006): 263, 278.

17. Cheryl Wittenauer, "Missouri Dismisses Dyslexic Executioner," *The Missourian*, May 2, 2007, http://digmo.org/stories/2007/05/02/missouri-dismisses-dyslexic-executioner/.

18. Wong, "Lethal Injection Protocols," 268.

19. Ibid., 266.

20. Ibid.

21. Ibid.

22. *Morales v. Tilton*, 465 F. Supp. 2d 972, 975 (N.D. Cal. 2006).

23. Wong, "Lethal Injection Protocols," 272, citing *Beardslee v. Woodford*, 395 F3d 1064, 1073 (9th Cir. 2005).

24. T. A. Zimmers, J. P. Sheldon, D. A. Lubarsky, F. Lopez-Munoz, et al., "Lethal Injection for Execution: Chemical Asphyxiation?" http://medicine.plosjournals.org/perlserv/?request=get-document&doi=10.1371/journal.pmed.0040156.

25. Wong, "Lethal Injection Protocols," 267.

16. Forfeiture

1. Raymond E. Brown, *The Death of the Messiah*, 2 vols. (New York: Doubleday, 1994), 2:953.

2. Ibid., 2:955.

3. Ibid., 2:956.

4. *Bennis v. Michigan*, 516 U.S. 442 (1996).

5. Ibid.

6. Janine Robben, "Losing by Forfeit?" *Oregon State Bar Bulletin* 67 (November 2006): 9, 14.

7. Amanda Doty, "Reshaping Environmental Criminal Law: How Forfeiture Statutes Can Deter Crime," *Georgetown International Law Review* 18 (2006): 521, 522.

8. *Dusenbery v. United States*, 534 U.S. 161 (2002).

9. Peter W. Salsich, "A Delicate Balance," *Saint Louis University Law Journal* 39 (1995): 585.

10. Robben, "Losing by Forfeit?" 9, 14.

11. Barry L. Johnson, "The Civil Asset Forfeiture Reform Act of 2000 and the Prospects for Federal Sentencing Reform," *Federal Sentencing Reporter* 14 (2001): 98.

12. James R. Humke, "Passing the Buck: An Analysis of *State v. Franco*, 257 Neb 15, 594 N.W.2d 633 (1999), and Nebraska's Forfeiture Law," *Nebraska Law Review* 83 (2005): 1299, 1318n117.

13. Ibid., 1314.

14. Brown, *Death of the Messiah*, 2:953.

17. The Problem of Innocence

1. Austin Sarat, *Mercy on Trial* (Princeton, N.J.: Princeton University Press, 2005), 3

2. Ibid., 6–7.

3. Ibid., 11.

4. Ibid., 25.

5. Ibid., 167–68.

6. Jim Dwyer, Peter Neufeld, and Barry Scheck, *Actual Innocence* (New York: Doubleday, 2000), xiii.

7. Samuel R. Gross, Kristen Jacoby, Daniel J. Matheson, Nicholas Montgomery, and Sujata Patil, "Exonerations in the United States 1989–2003," *Journal of Criminal Law and Criminology* 95, no. 2 (2005): 523.

8. Ibid., 552.

9. Interview by the *Florida Baptist Witness* with Jeb Bush, governor of Florida (Oct. 31, 2002), in Michael Rowan, "Minding Our Skepticism: A Conservative Approach to Capital Punishment," *Florida State University Law Review* 31 (2004): 377, 398n139.

10. Attorney General's Commission on Pornography, Final Report (Washington, D.C.: United States Department of Justice, July 1986), 1562.

11. Dwyer, Neufeld, and Scheck, *Actual Innocence*, xi.

12. Raymond E. Brown, *The Death of the Messiah*, 2 vols. (New York: Doubleday, 1994), 1:696.

13. David Dow, *Executed on a Technicality: Lethal Injustice on America's Death Row* (Boston: Beacon Press, 2005).

14. David R. Dow, "The End of Innocence," *New York Times*, June 16, 2006, http://www.nytimes.com/2006/06/16/opinion/16dow.html?ex=1308110400&en =29d4c137ef5545ff&ei=5090&partner=rssuserland&emc=rss.

18. Aloneness and the Ethics of the Crowd

1. Jane Daggett Dillenberger, *The Religious Art of Andy Warhol* (New York: Continuum, 1998).

2. *Tison v. Arizona*, 481 U.S. 137, 139 (1987).

3. Ibid.

4. Ibid., at 140–41.

5. Ibid., at 159 (Brennan, J. dissent).

6. Ibid., at 141.

7. Ibid., at 159 (Brennan, J. dissent).

8. 261 U.S. 86 (1923).

9. 481 U.S. at 182.

10. *Tison v. Arizona*, at 184 (Brennan, J. dissent).

SCRIPTURE INDEX

Old Testament

New Testament